I/F
±24

Fred Remembered

Recollections of John Shirley
Headmaster and Canon of Canterbury

Edited and with an introduction by
Robin Pittman

John Catt Educational Ltd.
Great Glemham, Saxmundham, Suffolk IP17 2DH
Tel: 01728 663666 Fax: 01728 663415

First Published 1997

by John Catt Educational Ltd,
Great Glemham, Saxmundham, Suffolk IP17 2DH
Tel: 01728 663666 Fax: 01728 663415
Managing Director: *Jonathan Evans* · Editor-in-Chief: *Derek Bingham*

The Sex Discrimination Act of 1975.
The publishers have taken all reasonable steps to avoid a contravention of Section 38 of
the Sex Discrimination Act 1975. However, it should be noted that (save where there is
an express provision to the contrary) where words have been used which denote the
masculine gender only, they shall, pursuant and subject to the said Act, for the purpose
of this publication, be deemed to include the feminine gender and vice versa.

ISBN: 0 901577 09 X

Set and designed by
John Catt Educational Limited

Printed and bound in Great Britain by
Bell & Bain Ltd, Glasgow

"He was a man of his word - we all knew this from the start - and his achievements at King's are still there, over three decades after his death, for all to see".

Contents

Foreword

Cardinal Basil Hume, Archbishop of Westminster

I am still not certain why I was asked to write this. I have no real entitlement to do so, save perhaps one. Fred fascinated me. When I was a schoolboy at Ampleforth stories about the headmaster of Worksop drifted northwards - yes, prefects wore funny gowns, rugby teams were beaten if they lost and, what was more, the headmaster had just moved south, taking boys and staff from Worksop with him. That had cost him membership of the Headmasters' Conference. As a boy that did not, of course, particularly concern me, but it was a good gossipy piece. I suspect that Shirley would have enjoyed that. I mean the gossip, not the expulsion. The latter, however, does not seem to have worried him too much - as a letter in this book explains. But Worksop had become a good school, and thanks to John Shirley. That much I knew.

Then later on, much later, I actually met Fred at King's, Canterbury. I used to take the Ampleforth rugby team to play King's at the beginning of the Christmas holidays. There I heard more stories: how fireworks, let off by the boys at the Deanery, had been encouraged by the headmaster to mark the launching of Sputnik; how the head rushed up and down the touchline during matches; how this or that distinguished person had been invited to the school. Then there were two memorable brief encounters, one when he told me that one day the RCs would get Canterbury Cathedral back again (yes, I realised that he was being facetious and not prophetic), the other when he gleefully told me that the Governors of the school could not remove him because they did not pay him.

What was Shirley really like? I read the contributions which constitute this book and came to admire the genius of a man who virtually created two excellent schools. Both, Worksop and King's, needed a man with drive, imagination and dedication. Shirley provided all three. Was he a genius? After reading the testimonies of those who knew him well and had been much influenced by him, I am inclined to think so.

This is what John Goudge says:

Two particularly strong impressions of Shirley remain with me: the first is the almost universal affection which he inspired and in which he was held; and the other is the aura of suspense he created around himself - when he appeared on the scene everyone stopped what they were doing, agog for what might happen and with heightened excitement.

And Shirley's only daughter writes this of him:

Devout, doubting, an ardent left-winger, a thorough snob, loving, self-centred, compassionate, hurtful, my father was, like anyone else, a mass of contradictions.

Indeed every writer in this book refers to one or more of these qualities. A man so described could never be dull. Shirley clearly was not. But he was as successful as he was colourful.

Two letters written by Shirley and quoted by contributors particularly impressed me. One in which Shirley tells the Lower Master how to be a good schoolmaster is recalled by Dick Prior:

It has seemed to me for many years... that the one right attitude of a master to his boys is that of humility - upon him has fallen by his choice the opportunity of directing his boys to the good life; and therein he will matter; not his brains nor looks, nor athletic prowess - himself.

The other letter was addressed to Michael Mayne, the future Dean of Westminster, on the occasion of the latter's ordination:

Never lose sight of Christ Who alone matters; don't let the institutional side of things obscure or distort Him.

In this letter Shirley, a Canon of Canterbury as well as a headmaster, says what I expect lay deepest in his heart. He knew about the things of the spirit as well as about the art of schoolmastering.

Teaching is a noble profession. Few endeavours can be more important than preparing young people for what the Education Act of 1988 describes as 'the opportunities, responsibilities and experiences of adult life'. Nor are there more important aims in the educational process than, as the same Act puts it, 'the spiritual, moral, mental, cultural and physical development of young people'. How successful Shirley was, only those who served under him as members of staff or the boys whom he influenced can tell. The testimonies given in this book witness to success, I believe. Yes, Shirley was a great headmaster. Nonetheless he was an eccentric - no bad thing in a teacher; an entrepreneur - such are often the ones to get things done; frightening and endearing alternatively, as it suited him.

Those who knew John Shirley will enjoy these reminiscences, and those who did not will learn about a man who could inspire both loyalty and affection - no mean achievement in any man, quite apart from the rest.

Preface

This is a symposium and neither a festschrift nor a biography. It is a collection of memoirs and opinions about John Shirley by those who knew him at various stages of his life. He was loved by some and not by others and the collection (arranged for the most part chronologically on the basis of the first meeting of contributor and subject) contains both praise and criticism. It reflects the man's complexity, and I have John Wilson (one of the contributors) to thank for the suggestion that this approach would, more vividly and effectively than a conventional biography, bring Shirley's remarkable personality before the reader.

Many facts about Shirley's life and career and the author's own assessment of his subject were brought together in David L Edwards's *F.J. Shirley: An Extraordinary Headmaster*, published in 1969. It is hoped that this present book will both complement and add to that earlier work, which appeared just two years after John Shirley's death.

I met Canon Shirley only once. Having in 1966 joined the staff of the King's School, Canterbury, I embarked on the task of completing the cataloguing of the books given to the school by Somerset Maugham. A small query arose concerning one volume and I was advised to seek the help of Shirley, by now retired from the headship for over three years, in solving it. I went without appointment to his Canon's residence at 15 The Precincts and was warmly received. The reason for my visit was courteously dealt with in five minutes, and I was then given a highly entertaining and vintage hour of Precincts gossip as he recounted the latest scandals and failings affecting the Cathedral and his colleagues on the Chapter. At the end he put his arm round my shoulder and saw me to the front door. The following morning I received a charming letter from him in which he put in writing the answer to my initial enquiry, wished me all good fortune and told me (as indeed it transpired) that he was not long for this world.

The memory and influence of John Shirley permeated King's during my 12 years there as a member of staff, and those who had taught under him seldom ceased to recount anecdotes of his *modus operandi* and of his more outrageous schemes and stratagems. When l became a member of the Headmasters' Conference 11 years after his death, the name of Shirley and his career at Worksop and King's were still frequent topics of conversation at bar and table.

I am very grateful to all those who agreed so readily to make possible the production of this book. The majority wrote their pieces and sent them on to me for editing and final agreement. Others allowed me to visit them and record our conversation. My wife generously and accurately transcribed the tapes, and I edited the results and submitted them to the contributors for their amendments and approval.

Paul Pollak, the King's School's archivist, deserves my special thanks. His knowledge of possible contributors and his continuing support for this enterprise were of the greatest help to me. I am indebted to him and to all the many others who have also given me the benefit of their advice, but I take all responsibility for the judgments and decisions made.

R N P

Robin Pittman taught at the King's School, Canterbury, from 1966 to 1978. He was subsequently headmaster of Queen Elizabeth's Hospital, Bristol, and of St. Peter's School, York.

Introduction

Robin Pittman

A few days after his death on 19 July 1967 his obituary in *The Times* described John Shirley as 'one of the most talked about headmasters in modern Britain' and added that he 'was also one of the most successful'. *The Times* went on to note that 'many anecdotes, most of them true, circulated about his unconventional methods', that 'he enjoyed talking and making money' and that 'he was ambitious and could be ruthless'. But the obituary was right to emphasise that these facets of his character were used to serve a purpose: 'his favourite activity was "getting hold" of a boy with moderate natural gifts, and pouring into him his own liveliness and singlemindedness'.

The first chapter of David L Edwards's *F.J. Shirley: An Extraordinary Headmaster*, is perceptive in its analysis of its subject's life and style: the perfectionist nature seen in the well-pressed suits, the expensive shoes, the cigars and fine claret; and his 'establishment' position as a residentiary Canon of Canterbury, a member of Brooks's and an honorary Fellow of his Oxford college. Edwards also paints a detailed picture of his character: the love of gossip, the elements of sulkiness and self-pity, the hint of self-mockery and his basic uncertainties perhaps stemming from some early sense of inferiority. The portrait that emerges also does justice to the essence of his achievements: to the boys as individuals 'he was the second father, the extraordinary man who had introduced them to the greatness and excitement of life'.

Shirley's entry in the *Dictionary of National Biography* also demands attention:

> The untiring competitiveness which he encouraged arose from his memories of his own under-privileged boyhood and slow start in life, and often amounted to a frank worldliness. But particularly in his later years, the style was so warmly human, and his devotion to the boys under his care was so evident, that he was loved as well as admired.

Frederick John Joseph Shirley was born the son of a carpenter in the Jericho district of Oxford on 24 February 1890. In his childhood and youth he was much influenced by the neighbouring Anglo-Catholic St Barnabas' church and attended its school before going on a scholarship to the City of Oxford High School. In 1909 he was admitted to St

Edmund Hall, Oxford, to read modern history while at the same time, because of his poor financial circumstances, continuing to live at home. Having gained second class honours in 1912 he went on to teach first at a Surbiton preparatory school and then as a sixth form master at a private school in Bedford. In December 1915 he was commissioned into the Royal Marine Light Infantry and subsequently, after ill health, into the Royal Naval Volunteer Reserve. While at the Admiralty he enrolled as a London University external student, graduated as a Bachelor of Laws and was called to the Bar.

In 1919 Shirley returned to teaching with an appointment at Framlingham College in Suffolk. During his time there he taught English and history, commanded the Officers' Training Corps contingent, became a housemaster and school librarian and, after ordination, was instituted as part-time rector of the nearby parish of Sternfield.

At the age of 35, in 1925, he became headmaster of St Cuthbert's College, Worksop, one of the poorest of the schools founded in the previous century by Nathaniel Woodard, and it was here that he was to find the opportunities for the development of his exceptional powers. He inherited an institution whose facilities and academic standards had only recently come under devastating criticism in a Board of Education report. Now under him the school's name was to be changed (to Worksop College) and its fortunes speedily improved: classrooms and laboratories were built, better boarding accommodation was provided, the grounds were expanded, examination and Oxford and Cambridge entry results were dramatically bettered, pupil numbers rose (213 in 1924 and 387 ten years later) and the whole life of the school - concerts, plays, societies, competitive games - was dynamically transformed. The *Dictionary of National Biography* sums up the Worksop achievement:

> Everything was stamped with Shirley's personality, which had become powerful and idiosyncratic. If governors of the school were cautious or pupils non-cooperative, they experienced wrath and a relentless drive; but parents and other visitors were charmed, and the boys were increasingly caught up in the excitement of an ambitious adventure.

In 1926 he married Dorothy Howard, the daughter of a company director, and they eventually had a family of two sons and a daughter. In 1931 he became a PhD(London) with a thesis on the sixteenth century theologian, Richard Hooker.

Perhaps the most controversial episode in John Shirley's career came in 1935 when he was appointed to the headship of the King's School, Canterbury, which at that time was badly in debt because of investment in the development of its preparatory department. Indeed the school faced closure before Shirley, with his record of what had been achieved at Worksop, was recognised as the person best equipped to save it. His appointment as headmaster was accompanied by his being made a residentiary Canon of the Cathedral, and this arrangement freed King's from paying him a full salary and allowed the head's house to be converted into additional boarders' accommodation. The most disputable aspect of his move to Canterbury was the translation at the same time of 30 or so Worksop pupils and several members of the Worksop teaching staff. This broke the code in such matters of the Headmasters' Conference and led to Shirley's suspension from HMC for a number of years, a manoeuvre that did him and King's little noticeable harm.

Now at Canterbury (where he became universally known as 'Fred') the success at Worksop was to be repeated but with appropriate variations. He first of all achieved a master-stroke: the Dean and Chapter would end their £1000 annual subsidy to the school and instead grant it a once-for-all lump sum of £26,000. It was this money that enabled him to embark on a major building and modernising programme. Further expansion resumed after the inevitable wartime pause and was to constitute in David Edwards's words 'an indelible personal monument... almost all conceived by Shirley himself'. He proved adept at acquiring leases from the Dean and Chapter on the most favourable terms and showed remarkable gifts as a fund-raiser and inspirer of successful appeals.

During the war, evacuation of the school to Cornwall (with the Choir School and St Edmund's School, Canterbury, also under Shirley's overall care) demonstrated further his skills of improvisation and unorthodox but effective leadership. He was to return to Canterbury in 1945 with more boys in the school than when he had left in 1940 (and with further work done on Hooker, which led to the subsequent publication of his *Richard Hooker and Contemporary Political Ideas* and the award in 1949 of an Oxford doctorate).

After 1945 the expansion of facilities and pupil numbers continued and the school's reputation for academic results, sporting success and musical accomplishment burgeoned. One of Shirley's great post-war achievements was the founding in 1952 of King's Week, an arts festival without equal in any other school and still flourishing decades later. In 1957 his huge building programme was crowned when the Queen Mother opened the assembly hall which soon was to bear his name.

No brief summary of Shirley's career at Canterbury would be complete without mention of his chequered relations with Hewlett Johnson, the 'Red Dean', who was *ex officio* the school's chairman of governors. There was a further up and down relationship with Field Marshal Montgomery (a boy at King's for one term) and more productive friendships with two other former pupils, Hugh Walpole and Somerset Maugham. He also cultivated links with the Royal Family and various royal visits over the years enhanced the school's prestige and standing.

After his retirement from the headship in 1962 at the age of 72 Shirley continued as a residentiary Canon and still held the posts of Librarian and Treasurer up to the time of his death five years later.

Janet Barlow (née Shirley)

Janet Barlow is the second child and only daughter of John Shirley and his wife Dorothy (née Howard). She was educated privately and at the King's School, Canterbury, and went on to read modern languages at Oxford. She married in 1950, has three sons and is a translator.

I have few very early memories of my father - perhaps at Worksop he was always busy in the school and my brother and I lived with our mother and such friends as Jack who looked after the carthorses (Jerry and Violet), Gertie who did the cooking and a series of nannies.

At Canterbury, however, he is memorable. Old enough now and at table with the family, I would hear indignant accounts of his battles with the Red Dean or other members of the Chapter (fights for justice often enough, protecting small tenants from sudden rent increases or an employee from dismissal), would hear of the demonic rivalries wilfully fostered by assistant masters, or of joyful plans for drawing in great men or great women to enhance the school's glory. Notables and royalty shone down all around us from signed photographs in silver frames. Or I might learn which building in or near the Precincts was next to be drawn into his creative grasp. (Archbishop Lang called him The Octopus, pronounced with the second 'o' stressed and long, an epithet my father seemed to find gratifying.)

My childhood was rich in that our house was much frequented by interesting and delightful people - singers, pianists, writers, generals - performers of all sorts, who came to entertain members of the school and naturally stayed with us. Conversation flourished, and I do mean conversation: my father was himself a brilliant talker but he knew very well how to encourage others and promote a flow of talk. With some guests no effort was needed - well do I remember my mother looking in despair at the full plates of A L Rowse and Lord David Cecil, while the rest of us sat round hungrily. We had finished; they were talking so hard they had not even started - did we get a pudding or didn't we?

Another desperate occasion was the time we were all so excited at a visit from General Montgomery, as he then was, that no one remembered to put any tea in the tea-pot and nothing came out of the spout but a stream of clear water. Guests politely failed to observe this, and, after a moment's consternation, we remedied the matter. This was just before D-day, and no doubt the General had other things to worry about. Later, when the war was over and the difficult peace beginning, Montgomery proved to be worth his weight in gold, for it was he, as a governor of King's, who got the boarding houses in Canterbury derequisitioned and the troops out of them, so that the school was able to return home from Cornwall. Later still Lord Montgomery of Alamein was found to be taking his role as governor all too seriously and would send letters to my father explaining to him how he ought to run his school. As far as I recollect, it was then discovered that a governor needed to clock up a certain number of attendances at meetings, in default of which his governorship would automatically lapse. Several governors' meetings then occurred in quick succession, at surprisingly short notice and inconvenient times.

Many of my memories of my father take us back far beyond my childhood to his own. He reminisced now and then, although some subjects were taboo. Once I asked him whether he had not found it difficult learning to speak what we now call standard English, when he came from a home where the speech was 'Oxford town'. (This accent I still dearly love, associating it as I do with my aunt and uncles.) All I got in reply was a savage "Yes!" and I knew better than to probe further.

His memory was better than mine ever has been. He remembered his Great Uncle Joseph, born in 1800, who died when my father was only three. Other memories of his: that his father brought up a family on £1 a week, that his mother, when a kitchenmaid before marriage, had seen a mouse fall into the soup cooking on the stove (did anyone eat that soup? I never knew), that he had had to clean the knives on Saturday mornings, a job he hated, that "*I* only had tuppence a week pocket money when *I* was a child!" (this in response, of course, to demands from me), that he had rheumatic fever twice in childhood and "they put down straw in the street". A sad memory going still further back: he told me that in his father's last illness, at a time when the old man had four grown children, each of them well able and willing to take care of him, his one terror was that he might have to go to the workhouse, where he had been long, long before as a child with his own family in a time of desperate need.

I am sure my father was spoilt. He was the youngest, a clever and no doubt charming little boy, doted on by his mother and his elder sister, my darling Aunt Florrie. She and his brothers were immensely proud of his success, and of each other. They all thought - *I* think! - that there is no one like us Shirleys. But I remember my Uncle Walter, eldest of those four, telling me seriously when he was over 90 that "my mother never really loved me, not like she loved Fred". I tried to persuade him he was wrong, but impressions made that early don't shift. Like my father, Walter had sung in the choir at St Barnabas', and used now to sit alone in his little house off the Iffley Road, running through a Gounod mass in his mind, or perhaps the Mozart Requiem. He was as gifted as

With Monty in Cornwall during the war. "Lord Montgomery of Alamein was found to be taking his role as governor all too seriously and would send letters to my father explaining how he ought to run his school. As far as I recollect, it was then discovered that a governor needed to clock up a certain number of attendances at meetings, in default of which his governorship would automatically lapse. Several governors' meetings then occurred in quick succession, at surprisingly short notice and inconvenient times".

his brother, but an eldest child doesn't have the same chances: Walter went out to work when he was 12 and little Fred was two. (He went to the Oxford University Press, where they took excellent care of their young employees, and where he had a long and happy career.) An eldest working-class child perhaps didn't even get as much food as a youngest - Walter was tiny, more than a head shorter than I am, whereas my father was five foot ten, an average height. He was called up three times during the First World War, was my Uncle Walter, and graded C3 and rejected each time - not expected to live long, as he told me gleefully, fit, well and in his right mind in his nineties.

Alfred, the second brother, ran away to sea when he was 11. By the time I knew him he was a lieutenant-commander, and I am ashamed to say that his exact duties were of less interest to me than the fact that during the 1939-45 war he used to send nylons from America for my mother and myself. Florrie left school "the day I was 13, and it was the happiest day of my life!" She made particularly good lardy cakes, I remember, and showed me how to make them.

What else can I dredge up? My father's schooldays - he was in a class, he said, of 100, all together in one place. They were divided into three sets and the master would teach one set while the other two got on with work they had been given. Everyone found this arrangement quite natural. He used to enjoy exams, he told me - something I could never understand! The only exam he ever failed, he said, was the Dip Ed, and he was told he would never make a teacher. He had a fine singing voice and was offered tuition at half-price, if he wanted to take up a musical career, but could not afford to accept the offer. I cannot be the only one who remembers him singing half a bar ahead of the entire school and congregation in the Cathedral when he thought things needed speeding up.

What with my own ill-health as a child and the complications of war, I had most of my education at home and at King's. My father compelled me to learn great quantities of poetry - I have forgotten most of it, but the rhythms stay with me. He taught me to write - how essential it is to spend time jotting down random ideas onto a blank sheet of paper and then find shapes and directions among the jottings before you let yourself even consider phrases. (That is how he wrote his sermons: he would write out the whole thing longhand, then reduce it to short headings, then reduce it again to a few lines on a half sheet of notepaper, which he would take into the pulpit, and never need to look at.) He taught me, with Latin, how to teach language - you offer your students short passages, easy, attractive, and let them triumphantly understand and enjoy these, before setting them to slog away at Kennedy. You slogged at Kennedy too, of course; no escape from that! He taught me, or tried to, to trust in the joyful love which God has for each of His individuals - 'It passeth knowledge, that dear love of thine, my saviour Jesus!' runs the hymn: words and a tune that stay with me, as they must with many an Old King's Scholar.

Devout, doubting, an ardent left-winger, a thorough snob, loving, self-centred, compassionate, hurtful, my father was, like anyone else, a mass of contradictions.

Tom Saul

Tom Saul was born in 1907 and went as a boarder to Framlingham College in September 1919. During his time there he won a gold medal for mathematics and represented the school in soccer, cricket and hockey. After leaving in 1924 he joined the National Provincial Bank, retiring in 1967 as manager of its Stevenage branch.

We always thought of Shirley as something of a sadist: he was very fond of the stick. He taught us history and English and was what I would call a 'crammer': he crammed it into you but you were always in fear of him. He always brought his cane into class with him; he would ask you a question - it was a matter of luck which question you had, some you knew and some you didn't - and if you failed to answer you were in danger of getting the stick. I used to hate his lessons.

Sometimes in Shirley's periods no history or English would be done at all; he would be on a completely different subject talking all the time. I remember one of these occasions very clearly: I was a lad who was somewhat behind on the birds and the bees, and he started talking about homosexuality, spending the whole lesson on the subject. I can recall the classroom, an old army hut, and him talking about this and asking the boys if they had any experience of it. Why he chose this particular subject for discussion was unknown but his purpose was probably to warn boys against the evils of adopting such practices. The discussions we had with him were varied. They went on for the whole period and little English or history was tackled. Another thing: he always had his favourites, and that did not help.

He had a peculiar habit when admonishing a pupil: he would come and stand round the back of a boy, get hold of his ear and just pull the earlobe. It was an extraordinary thing, twiddling the ears. I can never understand why he did it.

Shirley was a very good sports coach, both soccer and hockey. He was not a very good player himself but very, very keen; his methods were just pure 'go' and continual practice. When he became a housemaster he always wanted the house to be the top one. He also used to referee the football matches - he was a bit biased. We had a great rivalry with the town football side and I remember one occasion when the town brought a lot of supporters who lined the touchline and became rowdy and began to barrack. Shirley stopped the game and ordered them off the ground.

He was my housemaster (the house was called Maroon) for two terms before he transferred to Blue. What I recall most was his enthusiasm for his house to win the inter-house shield. Despite this, Maroon was top house for all my time at Framlingham.

Shirley became ordained while on the Framlingham staff. We didn't attend any service or anything like that; the whole thing was kept very quiet. He shared the chapel services with the chaplain and he was a good preacher. What else? He was connected with the cadets, helped with the debating society and also produced a Shakespeare play, *The Merchant of Venice*.

I suppose that he was quite gentle if you talked to him; the fear then went away. But I would not have dared to seek his help. His lessons were the ones we never looked forward to, and we worked harder because of his manner as he crammed it into us.

Denys Crews

Denys Crews went as a boy to Worksop College in 1927 becoming in due course Head of School House and a member of the 1st XV rugby team. From 1933 to 1936 he was at Emmanuel College, Cambridge, reading natural science. After Cambridge he taught for two years at Llandaff Cathedral Choir School before being appointed to teach biology at St Peter's School, York. During the war he was commissioned into the Sherwood Foresters and saw active service in North Africa, Italy and the Middle East. On demobilisation he returned to St Peter's and was made a housemaster. In 1958 he became headmaster of Scarborough College and on retirement in 1974 was for two years on the staff of the University of Hull Education Department.

After Colet Court I was destined for Bradfield College but Shirley's recruitment tours in the south of England changed that. He was wanting to alter Worksop's image (and disliked the way in which its pupils spoke). He was set on developing an entry from 'better' prep schools in the south, and my parents were tempted by Worksop's ridiculously low fees. My mother, who did not even know where Worksop was situated, was content that it was a Headmasters' Conference school, a public school of some sort. Thus we went to Swan and Edgars who supplied the uniform and, equipped with the required bowler hat (a typical Shirley thing), I was put on the train at Kings Cross for my first hard term as a new boy under him.

My first real encounters with Shirley were in my Latin lessons. I was put into the class for all the intelligent boys from southern schools and, being no scholar myself, found it absolutely hellish. Only one word can sum up Shirley's classroom manner - formidable. The experience of translating ten lines of Ovid early in the morning, with Shirley sitting on one's desk and with a cane down the sleeve of his gown, was to me terrifying. He dominated the lessons completely. I will admit that he was probably a good teacher; he seemed to be able to do it so easily himself. Here we were, however, aged 13 and always under the threat of the cane. It was this that was my first and very vivid experience of my new headmaster.

In Chapel too he was a commanding figure, a good preacher and extremely anxious that Worksop's choir, which I joined after a voice test, should be the best in the country. He would often come into the daily practices and sometimes take them over to ensure that the singing on Sundays would be perfect. He would also use the Chapel when he would summon groups of us during prep in the evening. There he would be in a black cassock storming up and down the aisle and berating us for our bad language. "I want anyone who has used a filthy word today to stand up," he demanded on one occasion. Nobody moved. Then the Head of School rose to his feet and he was followed by us all. Another time it was about our morals. "You're all abusing yourselves," he shouted. And then would follow a great tirade about the harm being done to ourselves and our souls. At the end of it he would sweep out; hopefully he felt better as we slunk back to prep or to bed. As a younger boy I saw this as a regime of fear; I dreaded being dragged out and made an example. In fact I was never humiliated in this way, but I had this fear that something awful was about to happen to me. He made us feel that we were all sinners and that the only way to a better life was to stop doing everything that came naturally to boys of our age.

Despite these summonses prep was a sacred time when we were all in our studies officially getting on with our work. I have vivid memories of Shirley wandering round the school during prep. He was a great smoker of cigars and I used to become terrified because one knew by the aroma that he was on the prowl nearby. With the cigar smoke wafting around him he would enter the study. The smell for me produced a sort of Pavlovian reaction: I associated it with both fear and the urgent need to get down to my work.

Shirley involved himself deeply in our sport and engaged in a fanatical quest for our success. I was a good cross-country runner and made the team. If we failed to win he would tell us how useless we were. He it was who prescribed our half-hour rests in the afternoon to digest our lunch and the cold baths in the morning. It was the same story with the rugger. He wanted Worksop to win every match and we had tours round the south of England (at some expense) to play schools considered more prestigious than our near neighbours. If on the tours we lost, then it would be straight into his study on our return to be harangued and abused for our failings.

On the touchline at home it was not uncommon for him to slash into the scrum with his umbrella. He was always tearing up and down in a rage. Of course he knew nothing about the game himself: for him it was just a matter of winning rather than losing. We were not playing for enjoyment; we were playing to win so that Worksop's prestige would be increased. It was similar with boxing. Shirley decided that house boxing would be good character training. We were paired off by weight and with no regard for skill (I was once knocked out and ended up in the sanatorium). This was him at his worst, at the ringside shouting and cursing me because I was falling over and letting down the house.

Another area of school life, which incidentally I dreaded, was drama. I remember having to sing a song at a house concert, with Shirley sitting in the front with his eyes blinking at me as I sang flat. He was himself a great actor: he could learn a part seemingly in a few minutes before going on stage, and if he forgot his lines he would extemporise. He would sit in the wings, with a whisky and a cigarette, come on well oiled and, with garments flowing, bring off a brilliant Shakespearean performance.

All, as I have said previously, was geared to enhancing Worksop's standing and repute. A big feather in his cap, which much impressed all the parents, was Shirley's engineering a visit by the then prime minister, Ramsay MacDonald, who arrived in goggles and flying helmet in a biplane which landed on the school playing fields. It was the same too with prestige facilities: everything had to be done well and to the highest standard. For example Shirley wanted to have the school library equipped with good antique furniture. He had a set of oak tables made and then organised a group of us to slash the surfaces with our corps bayonets. Wax was then rubbed into the scars and we thus had a library seemingly dating back centuries and in which we would take pride. This was Shirley at his most resourceful!

Shirley, as is clear, was a powerful personality. In my own case I did not battle with him; I did what I was told, possibly through fear. An element in his ability to dominate was this extraordinary habit of his in squeezing his eyes together and blinking at one - it was, for me at any rate, almost hypnotic. When I eventually became his head of house he and I never had a close relationship: I got down to my responsibilities and did not see him particularly often. I am not sure whether or not I was one of his favourites, but in some kind of way I was in awe of him. There was not only this penetrating stare - the feeling that he was looking right through you - but also his flaming temper, and it was this that I and others feared most.

But if I had no close affection for Shirley there was respect, almost a touch of admiration, for what he was attempting to achieve. His actions were invariably geared to his one ambition: the determination to put Worksop on top of all the public schools in England. The means to this end were of lesser concern to him. And besides the ruthlessness in him there was also generosity and care and a kind heart; many have testified to this. It was undoubtedly his efforts and influence that got me to Cambridge and, despite my having wanted to go into the Navy at 16 or become an engineer, steered me towards a career in teaching.

I have a final thought: when I reflect on my own headmastering career I cannot escape finding facets of it - ways in which I operated and performed - which undoubtedly originated from my schooldays at Worksop under this unique man with all his aspirations and his strange and frightening personality.

"A big feather in his cap, which much impressed all the parents, was Shirley's engineering a visit by the then prime minister, Ramsay MacDonald, who arrived in goggles and a flying helmet in a biplane, which landed on the school playing fields".

Joseph Dobbs

Joseph Dobbs was born in 1914 and educated from 1928 at Worksop College. He was a Scholar of Trinity Hall, Cambridge, and President of the Cambridge Union in 1936. He saw wartime commissioned service in the Royal Artillery and was mentioned in despatches. In 1946 he joined the Foreign Office, serving for many years in Moscow, latterly from 1971 to 1974 as Minister.

Of Shirley's many merits as headmaster one for me stands out: he took enormous pains to see that anyone who stood a chance of going to university, especially with a scholarship or exhibition, had the opportunity to do so. It was not just a matter of developing academic ability: many Worksop parents were far from rich and Shirley realised that financial back-up was as important as aptitude in Latin or science. Even with an open or county scholarship boys often had a gap to make up to meet the fees. Shirley knew all the channels to be explored, and he explored them to the limit. I am sure that we would have been embarrassed to learn what flattering letters he wrote about us to heads of colleges and admissions tutors.

In all this there was certainly a strong element of his own ambitions, but most of it came from his genuine interest in giving the boys the best chance for their own future. The numbers going up from Worksop to Oxford and Cambridge rose respectably in his time, and at Cambridge we had a flourishing OW Club and Shirley was almost always a guest of honour at our annual dinners.

Another of his great abilities touched the less bright as well as the brightest: we were all affected, to our great benefit, by his theatrical productions. He was a very theatrical man: if he had not chosen to be a clergyman and schoolmaster he could have made a great impresario or headed the firm of Shirley and Saatchi. His theatricalism came out in everything he did but especially in his role as producer of the annual school play. He would sometimes give himself a principal part as well - the Inquisitor in *Saint Joan*, for example, or Sir Peter Teazle in *The School for Scandal*. He put on *Saint Joan* very soon after my arrival as a new boy. Ever a man for a 'big name' he wrote and asked Bernard Shaw to come and see it. The school story was that Shaw replied with one of his famous postcards, declining the invitation and adding, 'Besides, I've seen it before'.

Other plays in my time were *Twelfth Night*, *Julius Caesar* and *Hamlet*. But the point is that in taking part in these and many other productions throughout the school we were unconsciously learning the practical use of the English language. I don't mean the adoption of a standard accent, but clarity and articulation, the feel of the language, absorbing things never taught in lessons. Now, of course, there are innumerable schools and teachers who achieve just as much in the same way; but in those days at Worksop we were very fortunate to have Shirley as producer, critic and goad.

Occasionally he would act quite out of character. He once bought a horse and took up riding. Two or three of us who had ridden a bit at home then had our chance. The horse had to be exercised when Shirley himself was unavailable. I was one of the lucky ones, and of course we had glorious riding country all round us. But I remember one time when Shirley had the horse but no saddle, and we had to ride bareback. I set off confidently for a point about a mile into Clumber Park; as soon as I turned round for home the horse took off, and it was not until we reached the hill leading up to the college that I regained control. The pleasures of exercising the headmaster's horse were matched by the perils.

Shirley's horsy period did not last for long, perhaps a year at most. And his horsemanship never came up to his high standards in other fields.

Thomas Stapleton

Professor Thomas Stapleton entered Milner Court (the Junior King's School, Canterbury) in 1929 at the age of nine years. He went to the Senior School with a Junior King's Scholarship in 1933. In 1938 he went up to University College, Oxford, to read medicine. After qualifying in 1943 he served in the Royal Army Medical Corps. He went to the United States of America on a Radcliffe Travelling Fellowship. For nine years he was at St Mary's Hospital Medical School and Paddington Green Children's Hospital. In 1960 he became Professor of Child Health in the University of Sydney and Director of the Institute of Child Health in Australia's Commonwealth Department of Health. In 1965 he was elected Secretary-General of the International Paediatric Association. He also served as Federal President of the Australian Institute of International Affairs. He returned to England in 1983 and in 1986 became President of the Paediatric Section of the Royal Society of Medicine. In 1965 the University of Sydney conferred on him the degree of Doctor of Medicine honoris causa.

I was already a pupil at King's when Canon Shirley arrived and could thus compare him with his predecessor, Norman Birley. My first observation was that Birley said "good morning" to the gardener as he passed by whereas Shirley did not. "That would have been a great sermon," my mother once remarked, "if one did not know what sort of man he is."

Like so many achievers in this world, he really put his heart and soul into any task he undertook. His rosy cheeks would glow as he went into a peroration from the pulpit. A contrast to the desiccated Canon Crum! He could not, however, approach the magnificence of the Red Dean, with his imposing figure, his white locks and his command of language. As Shirley's territorial ambitions grew, so did the problems with his Cathedral colleagues. They reputedly decided that never again should a King's School headmaster be a residentiary Canon and member of the Chapter, as Fred ran rings round them.

Shirley was a good publicist. "M'dears, we shall put all those with double-barrelled names in the programmes" - for the play in the Chapter House: *Hamlet, Richard of Bordeaux, Murder in the Cathedral*. And his stimulus at rehearsals was magnificent. A half-page photograph and a review in *The Times* were usual; no hiding under a bushel here! And there were the purple gowns (I never rose to the eminence which would have entitled me to wear one) and the court dress: all a bit ridiculous, but with a fine appreciation on his part of what would catch the public eye and, more especially, the eye of those with money.

Yes, Shirley liked inflicting pain - not in an evil way but because he realised that a nice stinging is often the simplest and quickest way to bring out the best in a boy - and fun for him too. He knew little about rugger but, striding up and down the touch-line, he gave great encouragement. "If you lose you will all be beaten," and they were. Amazingly no one regarded this as outrageous, but merely an emphasis on how everyone must strive to do even better than his best. He was good with money. "Better to have the collection on open plates than into little bags - seed the plate with a couple of notes and the others will follow." "The parents came pleading for a reduction in fees - not very sensible of them to park the Bentley outside my door."

Shirley was not immune from criticism. Dorothy Sayers came to one of the dinners that he gave for sixth form boys in his home. At the table he unwisely said that I should become a medical missionary. Miss Sayers retorted, "It is not for you to make a suggestion like that. The boy must make his own decision."

He could be unorthodox in his methods. Half the school down with 'flu, and at a few hours' notice there were buses to take us to the cliffs of Dover for a long walk to blow the cobwebs away. How sensible - and how upsetting to those lesser mortals who were merely conventional schoolmasters.

He was also an idealist. Many years after my time, there was his brave support from the pulpit of the campaign to prevent Bentley being hanged. This might have upset some parents who were major-generals, but it was a matter of principle which overrode fund-raising considerations.

Shirley made his errors. The Archbishop was to take an early morning school communion service. Fred said that there would be big trouble if there was not a good attendance. I went in order to see the beautifully embroidered robes, but I never took communion again. If it meant anything, it should make no difference whether the sacraments were given by an archbishop or a minor canon. I let him know.

I went to see him when he was close to death. The maid who opened the door said that he was too ill and not allowed to see visitors. "I am the doctor," I announced. He was delighted to see me and we had a great natter. While I was still at school he knew that I knew the faults in his character; I suspected that he knew those in mine. So, without a word ever being said, we had an eye-to-eye conspiracy of silence and deep understanding.

The world needs men like Fred Shirley. We are the poorer today for being so afraid to let exceptional men have their rein - and reign.

Tony Wortham

H P (Tony) Wortham went to the King's School, Canterbury, in 1933 and became Captain of School in September 1938. During the war he served in the Royal Army Ordnance Corps and was demobilised in 1946 in the rank of Major. He then went to Jesus College, Cambridge, where he read history and was elected a member of the Hawks Club. After teaching at two northern preparatory schools he went to Mount House School, Tavistock, becoming its headmaster in 1957 and retiring from that post 27 years later. He has a strong interest in ornithology, photography and dinghy sailing, and he travels extensively.

One of my first encounters with Shirley, our new headmaster, was at his installation as a residentiary Canon. I remember the person sitting next to me at the service turning and muttering, "He looks a pretty weak sort of chap, doesn't he?" It was not the most accurate initial assessment on his part!

My main contacts with Shirley followed on my being made Captain of School. Entries in my diary, 'Went to see Shirley', or, 'A long talk with Shirley', recur frequently. I saw him an enormous amount at the time and would keep him in the picture about all that was going on. This was for me an extra school year, and I gained so much from the responsibility of more or less running the school - he left a great deal to me. His trust in me and the confidence which this engendered has been a life-long benefit. A good example was when I received one of his little notes ordering me to report forthwith to Precincts 15, his Canon's residence. I went over straightaway and, as I walked in, he said, "Oh, Mr Maugham, this is Wortham; he's Head of School. Tony, will you take Mr Maugham over to lunch?" This was Somerset Maugham's first visit back to the school which he had loathed, and off I took him to the dining hall while Shirley stayed behind.

Also during that year Shirley asked me to be godfather to Charles, his younger and recently born son. My diary for the day of the baptism reads, 'Went to Charles Shirley's christening - I'm a godfather and so is Hugh Walpole'. Before I finally left school I went in January 1938 with Shirley and another boy, David Young, to Switzerland and then on, with Shirley alone, to Italy and Sicily. It was a sort of Grand Tour: we were sight-seeing each day, went to the opera in Rome and had a private car with a guide in the various cities. At Syracuse we parted: he put me on a train with a ticket to Dover while he himself went on to Malta.

The Duke of Kent opens new buildings in 1938. Archbishop Lang and Dean Hewlett Johnson (the Red Dean), chairman of the King's School governors, are behind.

Before the Lincoln's Inn Feast Society Dinner in 1939. Ronald Groves, who had accompanied Canon Shirley from Worksop, is on the right and Tony Wortham on the left.

During this year Shirley launched a scheme aimed at providing an endowment for the school, and the inauguration of it was marked by a Feast Society dinner in the hall of Lincoln's Inn. Ronnie Groves, ex-Worksop and housemaster of Walpole, drove Shirley, myself and two other monitors up to London for it. Shirley beforehand gave me the job of going round the tables at the end of the evening and collecting up all the cheques which would be written for the fund during the proceedings. On the way back, at about 1.00 am, I experienced one of my most terrible moments when Shirley turned in the car and asked me, "How much did you get, Tony?" Shamingly I had completely forgotten to do my collecting duty.

There is no doubting that Canterbury and his successes there had a mellowing effect on Shirley. But he was never able to cast off a certain element of self-pity. I have a letter from him, written in my last year at school, which, among other things, says this:

I myself have been hurt by very much this term. Some boys seem to regard me as an ogre, chiefly because I expect them to learn Latin.... Boys are often cruel, sometimes without knowing it. No man has ever laboured more self-sacrificingly than I have for this school, and that really means for you. In your inner selves you know that no man would espouse your interests as I would, and yet all that goes for nothing.

When I took over as headmaster of Mount House, so much needed to be done in developing the school, and I kept feeling that Shirley was behind me in what had to be tackled. I am absolutely convinced that it was his influence which enabled me to succeed. I almost felt that I was Shirley as I stood watching the bulldozers move in to carve out the playing fields.

After my parents he is the one person who truly influenced my life. Above all he had the remarkable ability to nurture one's self-confidence, and it was this that helped me immeasurably.

Alan Wilson

Alan Wilson joined the Junior King's School, Canterbury, in 1931, moving up to the Senior School in 1935. On leaving in 1940 he was commissioned into the Royal Signals and saw war service in India and the Mediterranean. He then read modern languages at King's College, Cambridge, and statistics at London School of Economics. During his professional career he was concerned with the business side of publishing (Reader's Digest *and* TV Times) *and was consultant to IPC Business Press and Verlag Das Beste, Germany. He was honorary secretary and treasurer of the OKS Association from 1958 to 1966 and a governor of the King's School from 1964 to 1974.*

John Shirley's arrival at King's coincided with my entry into the Senior School. In his first sermon as a Canon, delivered during the holidays in August 1935, he posed the question, 'Have we not something to learn from Russia?' and the all-city congregation formed the impression that he thought the answer was in the affirmative. In the light of their future rivalry it is interesting to recall the terms in which Dean Hewlett Johnson, the chairman of governors, had written to the parents some months before:

> We are full of hope that the School is to have a far more glorious history in the future than ever it has had in the past, wonderful though that history is, and venerable though its traditions are. Dr Shirley is among the outstanding men in the scholastic profession. Ten years ago he went to Worksop College, and has in that time made such a splendid success there that the Board of Education inspectors said that they could characterize it only as "phenomenal".

In this term there were five new masters and 64 new boys, including the 30 from Worksop occupying their new house in Palace Street. The latter, some of them almost six feet tall with two of them house prefects and playing in the 1st XV, already referred to our awesome new headmaster as "Fred".

At his first assembly Shirley outlined his immediate plans for the school and invited any boy to visit him at Precincts 15. Three weeks later, with Eton collar shining and all three buttons of my black coat done up (as required of fags) I took him up on this. Fred (we had all by now adopted the name) swiftly dispelled my trepidation, and as a result of my visit I was put up three forms into Remove. Weeks later he told the Remove that we would be entered for School Certificate the following July. The fact was that already, in a matter of weeks, it had become respectable to study one's books without being labelled a swot, and in due course our performance in the summer exams transformed the 1936 pass list.

Early in this first term Fred chose and cast the school play which he was to produce. He secured Mary Casson, cousin of the Thorndike brothers in my house (The Grange) and daughter of Dame Sybil, as leading lady, and for the first time the play was to be done in the Chapter House. Alas, the Chapter House lacked any access at the stage end and the powers that be were persuaded to have a door cut through from the Water Tower passage. After the performances we were thrilled to see reviews in three national newspapers and a half-page picture in *The Times*. Here was an early example of Fred's knack of getting good publicity.

And alongside play rehearsals he was also bundling his cassock and surplice into his Daimler 15 (the small one costing £465 - "I have to give them confidence without suggesting extravagance") and driving across to Thanet to preach at those prep schools which were failing to recommend King's to their parents.

At first Fred was not popular among the senior pupils: boys are conservative and suspicious of change; he had announced the abolition of our school uniform of which we were proud in favour of grey flannel suits; and he quickly became known as 'The Ogre'. At the end of this first term, however, he called a school assembly and spoke for over an hour. He was completely frank about the school's financial situation and the enormous difficulties which he and the school had to confront. He pleaded for our co-operation saying that without it all would be in vain, and he then went on to paint a heady vision of the future. It was a brilliant *tour de force*; the dropped pin could have been heard as he fired us with his own ambitions for King's, and there was no more talk of 'Ogre'.

On the final day of term a near-contemporary, James Gibb, was the last boy left in The Grange before catching his train home. As he walked into our scruffy and very inadequate loos he was startled, if not shocked, to find Fred there along with his secretary, Miss Milward. Even more surprisingly he handed him a hammer saying, "Come along, Jim, and crack some of these tiles and urinals. The governors won't let me have new lavatories, so I'm calling in the MOH [medical officer of health] to condemn them." Next term we had our brand new loos and baths (financed, in deference to the governors' edict, by a loan from Mrs Shirley).

Tony Eyre

Tony Eyre was a pupil at the King's School, Canterbury, from 1935 to 1940. He then went to Trinity College, Oxford, before service in the Royal Artillery. From 1942 to 1960 he was in the northern region of Nigeria, first with the Colonial Administrative Service and then with the Colonial Education Service. He then became editor for Longman's English language teaching division, retiring in 1985. He is the author of a number of books written for those learning English.

My first close encounter with Fred Shirley was a memorable one: a stormy Saturday afternoon, too wet for rugger; a few bob in my pocket from a recent birthday. Passing the Odeon I saw that *David Copperfield* was on and about to start. I slipped in, hoping not to be noticed in the dark auditorium. A vain hope. A voice breathed down my neck, "Have you your housemaster's permission? No? Then I'll see you in my study at eight o'clock." With a nasal chuckle it added generously, "You may stay for the film."

In his study a cane was laid out on a chair, but first he had to play cat-and-mouse. With his shrewd approach to personal relationships he needed to know what sort of boy he was chastising. He took my wrists, to draw me towards him and look me full in the face, and noticed at once that I wore no watch. He knew, from interviewing my mother at his London club (where she had been mesmerised by his puffs of smoke and the ash trickling down his waistcoat), that money was tight at home: he had promised her a scholarship of more than half the boarding fees (and I do not know to this day where the money came from). Now he quizzed me. No car, no wireless, no watch; every penny saved for schooling. That touched him. Our family's genteel impecuniosity was a far cry from the poverty of his own boyhood, but a fellow feeling could still make him wondrous kind.

His eye now fell on a copy of *Picture Post* lying on his desk. It carried an article on the Society of Genealogists with a full-page photograph of a man holding a scroll with the caption, 'Fourteen feet of the family of Eyre, a family worth belonging to'. When I confirmed that our tree went back to the Normans my stock soared. He promptly earmarked me as a programme seller for school plays and concerts, together with one or two others whose names he liked to see in print on the programme. Old family history appealed to his fancy (and an embellished pedigree of his wife's uncle, Lord Brocket, adorned his entrance hall). In the ensuing talk the cane was forgotten. It was past 'lights out' when I returned unscathed to report to my housemaster. As a Worksop man he showed no surprise; he knew his Fred.

There is a postscript to that evening. Shortly before the end of term Fred summoned me to his study and presented me with a handsome wristwatch. My parents were puzzled, but as I was totally unembarrassed they made no comment. Whence this generosity? Did it stem from his being as new to the school as I, and feeling his way? He was desperately keen to make friends, but boys naturally fight shy of overtures from authority, a matter of *timeo dominos et dona ferentes*. As time went on he overcame this resistance and got to know many boys very well. Perhaps I was just one of the first to respond, and perhaps he was grateful for it.

In those early years he liked to talk frankly, man to man, with as many of us as possible - partly to keep his finger on the pulse of school life and partly to test our reactions to his ideas. He seemed to derive encouragement from trying them out on us, whether we agreed or not. One favoured little group was bidden to breakfast with him and Mrs Shirley every day for a couple of months, ostensibly to improve their slightly spotty complexions with a strict Hay Diet, then the latest fashion in health food circles. It may have worked, but more importantly it gave him the chance to get to know them 'in depth' in a relaxed situation.

Confirmation classes were, of course, another opportunity. From his Worksop experience he knew how boys felt about religious observance. He soon saw that Cathedral matins bored us stiff with all its statutory psalms and dreary hymns and with its tedious lessons and sermons too often delivered by men with one foot in the grave. Instead he arranged our own services: early communion in the hush of the Crypt, matins in the Quire with rousing hymns and lessons read by the boys, evensong in the Crypt providing a peaceful end to an active day. His own occasional sermons were always electrifying. He was never pious. He had a broad vision of God the Creator, all-loving and all-powerful, and he struggled to express his interpretation of the *Logos*, the Word of St John's opening verse that was in the beginning. "The ultimate rationality" was his phrase, but he was happy to discuss my preference for Rupert Brooke's "the eternal mind".

To all the confirmation candidates in his first year he gave a booklet by Dorothy Sayers, *The Father Incomprehensible, the Son Incomprehensible, and the Whole Blessed Thing Incomprehensible*, which set out in simple language all the truths that we needed to know. For the eve of our confirmation he invited a little old Brown Brother from Hillfield Friary, near Cerne Abbas in Dorset, to talk to us in the Crypt. After the talk, each of us in turn had the chance to make our confession to him in a dark corner. When the old monk put his hand on my head in absolution, I felt a deep peace. Next morning Archbishop Cosmo Gordon Lang formally confirmed us in public pomp and ceremony at the high altar, but I told Fred later that for me the mystic moment had already come the previous night when the friar had blessed me. Never mind the Archbishop! Fred seemed quite moved. Though he revelled in pageantry he was an emotional chap, just as teenage boys are, to whom God is love, and love is an emotion that guides our doings, not an intellectual exercise. He knew that in bringing the Brown Brother he was supplying a need that no archbishop could fill.

My boarding house, Walpole, was new, a Shirley creation with a dual purpose: to bring boys into the Precincts from a small house on the edge of town which was closing, and to provide for the 30 Worksop boys whose parents held Fred in such high regard that they wanted their sons to follow him to Canterbury. For a while these two camps were chalk-and-cheese. As almost the only boy with a foot in neither, I was a source of neutral comment for Fred, who was anxious for his Midlands imports to be smoothly absorbed and to justify his decision to bring them. Thanks to his choice of housemaster, Ronnie Groves, a down-to-earth Yorkshireman (who was later to become head of Dulwich College), all went well once the teething problems were over.

The next summer Fred's friendship served me well. I went down with scarlet fever the night before the School Certificate exams and missed them all. He gave orders that I was to be treated as having obtained credits in all subjects, and this meant promotion to Middle VI and a house study. Thereafter I did my best to justify his faith in me by doing well in all exams; he knew how to foster loyalties in all sorts of boy by his personal interest and encouragement - even when he had to resort to chastisement to get the best out of them.

In my second year I came near to that fate again. Summoned in wrath to his study for some misdemeanour, I was saved by finding there an old friend of my father's from Keble days, Canon Bisdee. As a theological student he had been attached to St Barnabas' church, where Fred had been a choirboy, in the poorest quarter of Oxford. Canon Bisdee had been a powerful influence in his life and, recognising the boy's abilities, had inspired him to pursue his ambitions, fired by the same warmth of friendship as his protégé now displayed to us. Later as a priest there he had remained a source of strength to Fred and his family. So here he was, a house guest, invited to preach to us at evensong in the Crypt. Once more I escaped unscathed, even rewarded with a hug from Fred for being, through my father, already a friend of his much loved mentor.

To us boys he was always 'Fred', the name that came with him from Worksop. He had already dropped 'Joseph', his third name, because he

At the Norfolk cottage, with Janet, David and Mrs Shirley. Tony Eyre is at the back with Canon Shirley.

41

was uncomfortable with it - partly, I think, from dislike of 'Joe'. 'John', he is reported to have said, would sound better with a bishopric, if one ever came his way when his school mission was accomplished. Certainly 'Joe' would have been anathema to him when he crossed swords with the Red Dean, who worshipped Joe Stalin and was constantly visiting his hero or extolling his virtues from the top of a taxi at Speakers' Corner. Things came to a head when Hewlett Johnson started inviting sixth formers to political lectures in the Deanery, first one by Palme Dutt of the communist *Daily Worker*, and then another by Hannen Swaffer of the very left-wing *Daily Herald* - both dedicated to the abolition of independent schools. Soon Fred's phone was buzzing with protests from indignant parents. Whatever political leanings he may have had on coming to Canterbury, they were quickly subordinated to the school's need for support from influential people who would be unimpressed by the Dean's antics. Fred promptly put the Deanery out of bounds.

The Shirleys had a country cottage on the Norfolk coast and went there every summer. In my third year I was invited to join them for a week, together with another boy who was to be the following term's Captain of School. We were expected to accompany Fred on daily long walks visiting old churches. One day we were in disgrace for accepting an invitation to go mackerel fishing with another King's boy whose family also had a cottage nearby.* Fred had to walk to Trunch church alone and sulked the rest of the day. For such a powerful character he was surprisingly vulnerable. The next term I fell out of favour for a while, but the day came when we had to be measured for court dress, his extravagant notion for giving a touch of pageantry to the Upper Sixth on special occasions. I went round and told him that I was opting out (I refused even to mention the matter to my needy parents). For a moment we glared at each other. Then with a characteristic impulse of generosity he threw out his arms and clasped me: "Tell the school shop to put it on my bill; but when you leave, return it to me for some other boy."

Fred had a habit of questioning and then redirecting a boy's choice of career. In his astute judgment a would-be stockbroker might do better as a barrister, vet, priest, doctor or engineer, and sometimes the result was just as he had predicted. To my relief he approved my choice of the colonial service. In this I had two allies. The first was Lord Milner, renowned colonial administrator, whose name is perpetuated in Milner Court, the King's Junior School, and in the Milner scholarships for the sons of colonial civil servants (a fitting memorial to a man for whom Fred had great respect). The other, surprisingly, was Fred's own boyhood self. His favourite author had then been G A Henty, some of whose young heroes had followed the flag to distant lands, inspired by

* See also page 46

ideals of which Arnold of Rugby would have approved. Henty had been my favourite too, though it was Edgar Wallace's *Sanders of the River* that had tipped the scales. Now Fred said, "I've never had the urge to serve God's African children, as Livingstone did, but it pleases me that you should want to do so." So that was settled.

Long years after, I wrote to tell Fred that I was visiting Canterbury with a friend, Sheikh Sir Ahmed Awad. Might we call on him? "Come to lunch" was the reply. To my surprise the Captain of School met us at the station with a Rolls Royce and gave us an escorted tour of the school and Cathedral before joining us for lunch with the Shirleys. It suddenly dawned on me that, to Fred, a knighted sheikh had to be an oil magnate, good for a new pavilion perhaps or a block of squash courts. True, Awad was an imposing figure in his turban and robes, very tall and handsome and dignified, but he was chief justice of Northern Nigeria and no oil-rich prince. Far from blaming me for his misunderstanding and disappointment, Fred thanked me profusely afterwards for bringing "the most charming guest I've had for many a year." And he meant it. He hardly seemed aware that he had done me proud, beyond measure, with the gracious welcome that he and Mrs Shirley had provided for my friend.

Looking back, it puzzles me that nobody took the slightest notice when I or anyone else was on close terms with the head, sometimes round at his study late at night being talked to. He found me, a very ordinary boy and not one of your charmers, a 'good listener', and that was the root of his friendship. He had the constant need for a listener, as confidant or as sounding board according to his mood. No one was Fred's 'pet'. His study was an awesome place where one entered at one's peril, but every visit was an adventure, and boys thrive on adventure. I still have a picture postcard that he sent me from Naples - a handsome Greek bronze of a youthful *Mercurio in riposo*. It sat among the incoming Walpole house mail where anyone noticing the handwriting and bothering to read it would have seen: 'Been to Pompeii today - you ought to have been with me - good for your education'. That was Fred all over.

John Goudge

John Goudge was born in India in 1921 and was educated at the King's School, Canterbury, from 1935 to 1940. After war service with the Gurkhas he read modern history at Trinity College, Oxford. He was called to the Bar (Inner Temple) in 1958. In 1949 he joined British Petroleum and worked in both Iran and London. Since retirement in 1979 his occupations have included beekeeping, verse translation and writing.

I arrived at King's from my prep school in September 1935 at the same time as Shirley came from Worksop. One of my first encounters with him a few weeks into the term was when our paths crossed as I was collecting my bicycle from the sheds. I took off my hat expecting him to go straight on, but to my embarrassment he stopped and started talking to me as if we had known each other for years. The astonishing thing was that he knew my name!

Other arrivals that September were the famous 30 boys who accompanied Shirley from Worksop, with Walpole House inaugurated to accommodate them and their housemaster, Ronnie Groves, also a Worksop import. The story of this 'rape' of Worksop has often been told, and what was called 'spoliation' by some led to Shirley's being voted off the Headmasters' Conference. Many years later in 1964 Shirley wrote a justification of his actions, having been quizzed on the matter by the then secretary of the Old King's Scholars Association:

> I did not wrongly take boys from Worksop. In ten and a half years I had made that cheap and bankrupt school into a wealthy state: the numbers rose from 200 to over 400 (crammed); the fees from £90 to £150; I had built much more than half the school that stands, which, with modernising the rest, cost fully £100,000. My reign was from January 1925 to July 1935, included the slumps of 1928 and 1931 - when we went off the gold standard - and Worksop was the only school in the land to increase its numbers and raise its fees and build extensive buildings during those years. They were all formally opened - 'tho we began in 1927! - by the Prime Minister, Ramsay MacDonald, whose son Malcolm was a friend of mine, and still is, and is among my supporters for Brooks's. My grip was personal - I drew boys from all over England, whereas up to 1925 they'd all been Midlands and North - the parents thought the world of me, and when they knew in 1935 that I was going to Canterbury, many wanted their sons to accompany me. I discussed

this with the Worksop Governors who begged me to stay, offered me another 15 years' agreement with far more salary and a very large pension - and we had a formal agreement in writing that I was to have thirty and no more, that a large percentage of the thirty would be boys that had entered and not yet come, and that I would fill the places of all I took and leave W'sop with the numbers it would have had, had I been staying. This I did, and among my papers I have that agreement which will also be in the W'sop archives.

The style is familiar and his voice can be heard behind the written words. It seems convincing; but it cannot have convinced HMC. I find it hard to believe that he didn't quietly let it be known to certain parents that he would like their boys to go with him. Parents don't generally act in concert in the way he implies, especially the parents of boys who have not yet started at their chosen school.

Shirley used to do some teaching himself. He had written his own Latin primer designed to get dunces through exams. His teaching method - a mixture of threats and cajolements - was very effective. His classes were never dull and, although he could be beastly if he thought you weren't trying, he never stinted praise when it was earned.

Sometimes he would progress round the school in a seemingly random manner, checking up on masters and boys alike, so that you never knew he was coming. One day he would take over a Greek class; on another he spent the best part of an English period reading us the poems of Thomas Hood. It was as if, the evening before, he had happened to take down the book from a shelf in his study, enjoyed reading it and wanted to share the pleasure with us. His performance was electrifying - as it always was whether in classroom, at assembly or in the Cathedral.

I remember clearly Shirley's harangues to the school in assembly. Sometimes it was just a lesson in manners following an incident which had incurred his wrath, but more often in my (and his) early years his subject was the perilous state in which the school found itself. He made no bones about it: it was almost broke, he was doing what he could to pull it together, and we must do our part, acting as ambassadors, backing him and, above all, passing examinations and winning scholarships and matches. We emerged from these occasions dazed by his eloquence, and his passionate appeals welded us together and inspired a strong corporate spirit.

Stories about Shirley's dramatic antics are legion. At Worksop, we were told, having selected a play for the drama society to perform, he would stand back and let the staff and boys get on with it until about a fortnight before the actual performance, when he would turn up unexpectedly at a rehearsal and announce that so and so was 'hopeless', and, as it was far too late to find a replacement, he would have to take the part himself. It would be one he had had his eye on all the time, and not a minor part either. At Canterbury I saw him as the gardener ('yond dangling apricocks') in *Richard II* and he dominated that short scene as Shakespeare surely intended. But his interventions were not always successful. On one occasion he so flustered the cast of *Sir Thomas More* (his own edition of the play reputed to have been partly written by Shakespeare) that they went through most of one scene twice - and it wasn't a rehearsal. The reason was his over-generous helpings of claret administered beforehand to get them in the mood. In that production the boy playing Lady More had been absent from a couple of rehearsals with stomach trouble, and after the final one Shirley threatened him, "If you get a bilious attack on the night, I'll get a ten-foot red tube and clean you right out." (Was he thinking of the discomforts of the colonic irrigations which rumour claimed he received on visits to London?)

In 1937 Shirley bought a cottage in the village of Happisburgh on the Norfolk coast. This was a potential embarrassment to me because my parents took a summer cottage from 1935 to 1939 in the same place, and we used to move there at much the same time as the Shirleys came from Canterbury. Although I never wavered in my liking and respect for him, his presence was a constant reminder of school, and it seemed 'a bit thick' to have him there in the background for half the summer holidays. But in fact after I had paid a courtesy call and been asked to tea, I didn't see much of him, and I don't think that my parents entertained him. (My mother used to get on well with him; they respected each other and each recognised the other's strengths. My father also respected him, but I believe he thought him rather 'vulgar'; there was in him an element of this, evidenced by the way he used to boast of his achievements and of his contacts in high places. This was distasteful to my father's quiet and unassuming nature.) Shirley would have King's boys to stay in Norfolk for a week or so. He liked long walks and expected his guests to keep him company. Sometimes the atmosphere would become strained, and they used me as an excuse to escape for a while, spending an afternoon with us on the beach.* There was one advantage of his proximity: he received details of all the examination results and summoned me to see my own. I was thus the first boy in the school to know exactly how I had done.

During my time at King's beating - by headmaster and monitors and occasionally by housemasters - was a common practice. I was caned three times, and the last occasion was bizarre indeed. By then the school had been evacuated to Cornwall, and another boy and I, both in our last few weeks before leaving, had spent an afternoon and evening being entertained - a generous tea and a couple of cigarettes each - by a

* See also page 42

member of staff who had rooms in a neighbouring village.

We were late in getting back and Shirley saw us. After we had gone to bed we were summoned to see him. He taxed us with slackness and setting a bad example and challenged us to deny we had been smoking. Neither of us bothered to do so. Having given us a lecture, he announced that he was going to beat us; we could, if we wished, refuse to submit, but in that case he would expel us. This threat in the circumstances was quite unreasonable. We didn't believe he would carry it out, but we hadn't the nerve to call his bluff. Not wishing to provoke him or prolong the matter, we agreed to take the beating. The room was full of furniture - cupboards, a table, chairs, bookshelves and a bed. There simply wasn't room to swing a cane properly, so each of us in turn had to bend over the bed and was beaten, gently - 37 strokes. It didn't hurt at first, but the cumulative effect was considerable and the pain towards the end excruciating. We hadn't been expecting anything like it and the shock was severe, not least because of the calculated and cunning way in which it was done, carefully planned in advance and indicating a measure of sadism. There was no passion or anger apparent and curiously neither of us afterwards felt any grudge. I think the reason was that each of us at heart liked Shirley and we knew he liked us.

In my time at King's Shirley was in his early middle-aged prime. His appearance left one in no doubt that here was an exceptional man. He was of medium height and build with a slight hint of a paunch, and his feet and hands were small, almost delicate. His suits were expensively tailor-made and in perfect taste, with his shoes always highly polished. His complexion was florid and his lips full. His eyes were grey, and his hair was also grey and rather sparse. He had a curious habit of blinking as he looked at you - not a myopic blink (though he always wore glasses), but it almost seemed as if he were punctuating his sentences with his eyes. His voice was pleasant, powerful when required, always audible, and when he spoke to you his words were often preceded by a pursing of the lips and an exhalation through the nose, accompanied by a kind of humming sound which could be taken as a sign of approval, astonishment, ridicule, disbelief, amusement or anger, depending on the circumstances. He smoked cigarettes but didn't deliberately inhale; in fact he rarely took the cigarette out of his mouth, preferring to let it burn and allowing the ash to drop on his waistcoat.

He never talked down to us; we were astonished at how he treated us as equals. Many of us weren't equipped to deal with this. He seemed to be thinking aloud and at the same time seeking sympathy. Usually no response was demanded and we simply listened in wonder, flattered by his confidences. His normal form of address was "m'dear". He was genuinely fond of the company of boys. He may have been a lonely man with associates too wary of his power of personality ever to become intimate. Perhaps he lacked the real friends that most of us need to confide in and trust, and met this need to some extent by talking to his boys. If there was any homosexual element in this relationship it was completely under control and we were not embarrassed by it.

Two particularly strong impressions of Shirley remain with me: the first is the almost universal affection which he inspired and in which he was held; and the other is the aura of suspense he created around himself - when he appeared on the scene everyone stopped what they were doing, agog for what might happen and with heightened excitement. And then there was his energy: establishing valuable and lasting contacts with eminent people, getting them to use their influence for the benefit of the school; and at the same time managing to carry out the pastoral side of his calling in a way that would have filled the day of any ordinary man. Then there was the teaching as well. No one could have done all this without a degree of ruthlessness, without arousing jealousy and making enemies. And he was ruthless, particularly with his staff whom he regarded as expendable (whereas the boys were not), and he brooked no opposition - no one stood in his way for long. We witnessed the occasional injustice; tantrums too; childishness even, at times. But he made us all feel vibrantly part of what he was doing, and few leaving in my year can have regretted their time at King's or failed to feel proud of their association with such a man - and to be the richer for it.

John Williams

John Williams was a chorister at the resident All Saints' Choir School, Margaret Street, London, from 1930 to 1935. He went in that year as a music scholar to the King's School, Canterbury, and proceeded in 1939 to St John's College, Cambridge, as a choral scholar. During the war he served as an officer in the Royal Naval Volunteer Reserve. Subsequently he was organist and choirmaster at All Saint's, Margaret Street, a professor at the Royal College of Music and Master of the Music at Her Majesty's Chapel Royal within the Tower of London.

The year was 1935 and I was seated with my parents in Dr Shirley's study at Worksop being interviewed for my possible entry there in the autumn. The Depression of the early thirties made money a scarce commodity, and money was very much to the fore in our conversation on that day; my father could not possibly pay all the school fees and my entry depended entirely on my securing one of the music scholarships available. It is firmly printed on my memory that Shirley made the remark that "a businessman cannot be honest", this provoking an argument with my father. Perhaps this observation revealed something of his character and accounted for some of his more controversial actions.

The conversation then turned upon how Worksop College had been fortunate in having the financial support of the Duke of Newcastle, a familiar name to me as a chorister at All Saints', Margaret Street, where he was a member of the congregation and a strong supporter of its choir school. Thus the benevolence of the Duke and the topic of Anglo-Catholicism provided common subjects for both parties.

Shirley, at that time, was a long way ahead of his contemporaries in regard to the part that music should play in a school. He realised that boys with good treble voices and musical experience from reputable choir schools would, in due course, provide the altos, tenors and basses for the choir and, sometimes, instrumentalists for the orchestra. This idea he had already been putting into practice at Worksop with some success, and it was to be the same policy, followed later at King's, Canterbury, which produced even greater results.

Fortunately for me, this initial interview proved positive and a music scholarship was forthcoming. Perhaps my five years' training in the Anglo-Catholic hothouse of All Saints', Margaret Street, was an added advantage since Shirley was very much of that persuasion in his churchmanship. His methods in conducting the interview could not have been faulted, but more controversial were some of his unorthodox means of recruiting suitable boys. In the economic climate of the time pupils were at a premium and headmasters were up against fierce competition in filling their places. Some of the stories in this respect concerning Shirley were possibly apocryphal, but nonetheless characteristic of the man. One such concerned a conversation in a train compartment between Shirley, by then at Canterbury, and a mother taking her son back to his school. In the course of the conversation Shirley is reputed to have asked the mother how much her son's school was giving for his scholarship. On receiving the answer he then offered a larger sum if she would consider sending her boy to King's. The start of my own school career under Shirley was to be not entirely dissimilar.

After the award of my Worksop scholarship everything, from my parents' point of view, seemed to be satisfactory: Shirley came across as a successful headmaster with the interests of the boys very much at the centre; there seemed to be no stuffiness or dead traditions in dress or teaching; the picture was painted of a happy school based on firm discipline (with some use of the cane but not delivered by school prefects); and, to my father's intense delight, there was definite religious teaching with an Anglo-Catholic bias. And there was also Shirley's smile and slight teasing manner which left me somewhat nervous as to what to expect the following autumn. (These characteristics were to become endearing after a couple of years and even more so after my leaving school.)

Then, early in that 1935 summer term, a letter arrived at the All Saints' Choir School with the surprise information that Dr Shirley was being translated to the King's School, Canterbury, in the autumn. It also contained an offer to my parents that I could go to King's with the same music scholarship as had been awarded me at Worksop. This was accepted readily by all concerned and I duly started at King's in September. At the time we were delighted with this deal, and it quickly transpired that Shirley was also bringing some 30 boys and three masters with him from Worksop to form the nucleus of a new house - to be named Walpole after the well-known writer who had been at King's as a boy. In charge of the house was to be Ronnie Groves, one of Shirley's great admirers and already a very experienced Worksop housemaster. And it was this transfer *en bloc* from north to south that was to lead to Shirley's eviction from the Headmasters' Conference. His expulsion is the one fact about him known throughout the public school world, and perhaps he may have been too harshly judged by many headmasters then and, indeed, since. Did they not have a certain feeling of envy? And how it affected Shirley himself is a matter of conjecture; it did not deter him from forging ahead with his plans.

The school which I and this Worksop headmaster now joined was in a bad state financially and scholastically; numbers had dwindled; it had the reputation of being a school with the characteristics of those immortalised in nineteenth century novels - fagging, bullying, compulsory sports at the expense of the arts; music of any standard did not exist; compulsory attendance on long and dreary occasions in the Cathedral was the lip-service paid to religion. With regard to this last, Shirley effected speedy change: attendance at Cathedral services was cut to one per month and later abandoned; the school eventually had its own matins in the Cathedral, with its own musical director and choir and with the long boring preaching replaced by sermons that were shorter and more lively.

At the start and unlike Worksop, King's had no choral or instrumental scholarships nor a music tradition of its own. Thus, by a lucky chance, I had become the first boy at King's from a choir school to receive a major scholarship. In the coming years Shirley was to enlarge his net to many more such schools as well as taking more boys from All Saints' as they became available.

What then of this remarkable man? He was 'liberal' in his thinking and a firm opponent of the dead hand of tradition. He was also a hard taskmaster. He expected good results and his own teaching in his unorthodox Latin class is a good example of this: a certain fear was always present, also a healthy respect, with all never in doubt as to what was expected of them. Nor were his methods always perhaps the kindest. In my own case, for example, I was promised a 'leaving scholarship' only if I achieved Higher Certificate and an Associateship of the Royal College of Organists. Both these examinations were to take place in my final year. The bargain may not have been entirely ethical, but it worked!

After leaving King's I looked upon Fred as a real friend. Three years at Cambridge and over four as a RNVR officer in corvettes left little time for us to meet, but we did correspond on occasions. Once, with me still in uniform, an unsolicited visit to him in Canterbury renewed our contact but on a different level. The encounter had its slightly roguish qualities. Knocking on his door in the Dark Entry I was informed that he was not available, but my expression of disappointment (or was it the sight of my naval uniform?) must have had some effect and I was told to wait. Mrs Shirley then appeared, we had a fond embrace and I was invited in and asked to go upstairs, there to find Fred reading in bed. We had a very diverting conversation about all the scandals and gossips in the Deanery and Cathedral (its "boring music, too much of it Tudor"). He was genuinely pleased to see me, keen to know all about life in small ships and concerned about my future after demobilisation, giving me some helpful advice.

He kept in touch with many OKS and in my case sent me letters of support and congratulations on new appointments and personal events such as marriage or deaths. He even found time in a busy life to come up to London and christen my eldest daughter. He encouraged Old Boys to pay him visits from time to time, and these were always diverting occasions and full of gossip and scandal. He once told me that he had a greater affinity with the 1935-9 vintage of boys than those coming during and after the war: we had been at the school when he was really laying the foundations for future success. Many years later, at his last attendance at the OKS dinner, he spoke at some length as to how he had planned and put into effect the huge building programme of that early period, informing us quite openly of some of the devious methods which he had employed to find the money. If he came over on this occasion as a despot, then he was a very benevolent one, and he received prolonged applause as we sensed the passing of an era.

Those of us who came under this man's influence, be it as schoolboy or friend, always found him stimulating and provocative. What stand out are his single-mindedness and his clear vision of what a school should be. The understanding of what makes schoolboys tick was another natural gift. Religion was to be at the centre, but its practice was to be made acceptable and never forced down with humbug and Victorian thinking. He was a man of his word - we all knew this from the start - and his achievements at King's are still there, over three decades after his death, for all to see.

James Breese

James Breese was a pupil at the King's School, Canterbury, from 1937 to 1942. From there he went on to Trinity College, Oxford, and subsequently for 23 years taught classics at various schools, during which time he took a further degree in psychology. Then for 14 years he was a senior lecturer in education at Goldsmiths' College, London. After retirement in 1984 he worked voluntarily for the Guild of Health (the Church's Ministry of Healing) and from 1988 was its chairman. He died in 1996.

Fred, like the rest of us, had many sides to him; but in his case they were publicly disclosed. Whereas others conceal the 'dark' aspect of their souls, with only those closest to them aware of their secret characteristics, he had the self-confidence (or was it the impudence of the small boy in him?) to reveal himself 'warts and all'.

I have two clear memories of the worst side of this remarkable man. The first was in 1938 when I was a member of his Latin set. It was an afternoon lesson, and two of the class had displeased him in one way or another. He caned both of them hard in front of us all. At the end of the period I made for the lavatory, my emotions churned up and my stomach bearing the physical brunt. The second was years later when I was teaching in one of Kent's other public schools. Staff there were talking about a match at which Shirley had been on the touchline. The head of the opposing school had invited Fred in for tea, but King's lost and Shirley stormed off in a tantrum. It was an instance of such extraordinary bad manners that I blushed for him.

If these are the warts, then they are more than balanced by the other facets of his character. There were his devotion and dedication to not only saving King's from extinction but also making it a leading school, and what he did here has been well publicised. What perhaps is less known were the humility and anxieties of the man. By 1942 I was a monitor, and Fred would hold monitors' meetings late in the evening. At these he would talk about himself, his health worries, his feeling that he had achieved little in life and his other concerns. Isolated as many at the top are, he yet had the openness to use these gatherings for a mixture of the confessional and a group therapy session when that kind of disclosure of inner feelings would more usually be displayed. He showed us the man behind the mask and was not afraid to bare his soul. Over the years I have learned through my counselling work to be open about myself when appropriate; it was Fred's example in these evening meetings that made me realise that such disclosure was safe. Here was a headmaster with a reputation for dynamic and ruthless behaviour, outwardly tough, demanding, even cruel, and yet showing the soft centre, revealing the anxieties and worries which others conceal for fear of losing face.

Then there was Fred, the experimenter with the unusual. Early in 1941, some months after the school's evacuation to Cornwall, he, a '20 a day' man himself, became so concerned about the amount of boys' smoking that he suggested a bargain: he would give up for a term if the boys involved would do the same. I believe that he stuck it out for ten weeks but cannot recall whether it was he or some of my contemporaries who cracked first. At least his challenge had some effect.

Finally there was the Fred who was always interested and concerned and who made us feel that every pupil was important to him. For example, I was about to fill up entrance forms for Cambridge and took them along to him; within half an hour I was entered for Trinity College, Oxford (and ultimately successful). I forget now what his reasoning was, perhaps just prejudice, but it was his consideration and involvement that I recall. And there was also his flexibility: it was rumoured that in those war years no parent ever paid the same fee. In my case, with a small scholarship, my father was asked to pay a fee as if the award were somewhat larger. It was an instance of his understanding and concern and of his having no fear at being unconventional. There was a benevolence in this dictatorial man!

Was he, this Reverend Headmaster and Canon of Canterbury, a proper Christian? He never made a secret of the difficulties in combining the acumen of a successful businessman (which as a head he had to be) with the honesty and morality demanded by his religion. I believe, however, that the life and teaching of Christ meant much to him, and I recall one of his sermons in which he stressed the soul's as well as the body's need for nourishment. His ambitions were for the school and its pupils and not for himself. He was serving a cause rather than glorifying in any personal self-advancement. If on occasions he fell from grace he had it in him to seek God's forgiveness with a fervour greater than that of lesser mortals. He totally lacked the self-righteousness of the Pharisee and in the end deserved the Almighty's favour.

Hilary Groves

Hilary Groves is the widow of Ronald Groves, mentioned by various contributors in this collection and one of the Worksop College members of staff who came to the King's School, Canterbury, with John Shirley in 1935. She married her husband in 1939 and took over the matron's duties in Walpole, the house founded in 1935 to accommodate the boys brought from Worksop and of which he was housemaster. Her husband subsequently became Headmaster of Campbell College, Belfast, and, as had been his wife's father, Master of Dulwich College.

When I told my father that Ronald and I were thinking of getting married, he did not at first approve. Having been a headmaster himself he knew that Shirley had been temporarily struck off the Headmasters' Conference for taking boys and masters with him from Worksop to Canterbury and doubted whether Shirley would be a good influence on his future son-in-law. When he got to know Ronald and the situation better, he overcame his hesitation and agreed to the marriage.

Knowing my father's views, I started out with a prejudice against Shirley, and at our first meeting I did not change my opinion. This was at a tea-party after a cricket match when he treated his wife most discourteously, slapping her down with a display of less than good manners. Mrs Shirley seemed to tolerate this. I later got to know her and found she was a very good, gentle person who generously used her own financial resources to help the school.

The atmosphere between Shirley and his staff was often tense. He had one goal - to rescue King's (which he did) - and it would be fair to say that he trampled on those who got in the way of this. The relationship between him and Ronald, however, was different. Ronald was an admirer of Shirley. Their upbringings had been remarkably similar; both had backgrounds which were relatively humble. Ronald's father was a builder and contractor who hoped that his son would follow him into the business, but Ronald decided he wanted to teach. In 1932 he went to Worksop where Shirley made him a housemaster and supported him greatly - hence Shirley's invitation for Ronald to accompany him to Canterbury. I do not believe that at the time Ronald saw anything unethical in deciding to go; his father's advice was that Shirley had been good to him and that, therefore, he should do what he could for Shirley in return.

After the translation to King's their working relationship continued to strengthen. Ronald, with his specialised family knowledge of building and contracting, was of particular value to Shirley; so in a short time he was not only a housemaster and senior science master but also bursar. This was certainly one way for Shirley to economise on a bursar's salary.

Another key man behind the scenes at the school was Harry Curtis. He had started at King's many years before as a bootboy. After promotion to Steward he became one of Shirley's right-hand men. Curtis's role was vital to the school's success; he was very good at his job and knew more about Shirley than most. Shirley was never in awe of anyone; neither was Curtis. This is neatly illustrated - as retailed by Curtis - by what happened when a music master went to Shirley's study one day in order to request some money for instruments. When he entered, Shirley and Curtis were evidently deep in business of some sort, and he offered to come back later. "No, no, old man," said Shirley, "Come on in." He entered and listened to the two men discussing the proposed acquisition of a near-by house for the school. A hitch had arisen in the negotiations. "Well, then," said Shirley to Curtis, "We'll have to go to court and you'll have to go into the witness-box and swear that the house is being used for immoral purposes." "Not bloody likely," replied Curtis. "Oh well," said Shirley, "We'll have to think of something else."

When Ronald left King's in 1943 for Campbell College, Shirley - in addition to being headmaster - took on the job of bursar himself. Ronald continued to be guardian to a boy who was still in Walpole House; he therefore still received Shirley's *Notes to Parents*. In these *Notes* he was astounded to read how successful the new bursar had been in saving money on the school's heating bill. In fact the truth was that Ronald had been aware of coming shortages and had had the foresight over many months to accumulate a huge pile of coke. Shirley had been using this pile and saving money. Being 'economical with the truth' is part of any entrepreneur's technique. Shirley was a very good entrepreneur.

Undoubtedly Shirley's ways of operating influenced Ronald in his career as a headmaster. Some of these Ronald adopted; others - such as Shirley's punishment methods - he rejected. For instance, at Dulwich he introduced the practice of regularly inviting excellent outside speakers to the sixth form, an admirable practice that Shirley had started at King's.

Over the years after our move from King's the two of them kept in touch. Indeed, one of the first letters that Ronald received at Dulwich was from Shirley asking for a rugby fixture. He had to wait a year or two.

The fact is that Shirley was very much a two-sided man; there was a charming side where he was extremely good with the boys, and there was another side which was motivated by ambition. He is reputed to have said early on in his career that he had three aspirations: to become a successful headmaster, to marry a rich wife and to be made a bishop. At least he managed two of them.

Dick Prior

R H Prior (known during his Canterbury years as 'Sam') read mathematics at Christ Church, Oxford, before entering the teaching profession. He was on the staff of the King's School, Canterbury, from 1939 to 1960, except for the war years when he saw service in the Royal Air Force, gaining the Distinguished Flying Cross and retiring in the rank of Wing-Commander. From 1960 to 1963 he was headmaster of a boys' boarding school in Nigeria and then, from 1964 until his retirement in 1976, headmaster of Oxford School (founded in 1966 by the amalgamation of Southfield School and the City of Oxford High School, where at the latter John Shirley had been a pupil).

In 1937, having achieved my Oxford mathematics degree, I started to apply for teaching posts and, with unemployment very high, the best I could get were one or two temporary jobs. Early in 1939, having just about abandoned hope for anything permanent, I saw an advertisement for a post at King's, Canterbury, and put in for it. A telegram quickly came back: 'Glad to see you on Friday or Saturday. Headmaster, Canterbury'. I replied at once and went for my interview with Canon Shirley. I well remember his welcoming smile which gave me much-needed confidence, and I remember too our chat which included, for some odd reason, a discussion about infant baptism. After the senior housemaster had taken me round the school, I was brought back to Shirley who, after another short chat, suddenly said, to my great surprise and delight, "Well, old man (he always seemed to call me 'old man'), I think I'd like you to come." I agreed without hesitation and my whole future career started from that moment.

The brisk way in which I was appointed was typical of the man: John Shirley never wasted time but got straight on with the job in hand. This was well illustrated by what he had achieved within a few years of his arrival in Canterbury; an enormous amount of building and general re-organisation had been accomplished. It was also evident in a memorable school assembly in 1940, just after the battle leading to the fall of France, when he suddenly announced that the boys should all go back to their houses and pack, as they were to go home that morning and meet again in 14 days' time at Carlyon Bay Hotel in Cornwall.

Shirley was thus a wonderful person for tackling matters and not dithering, and one reason for this was his great faith in God's guidance which was liable to come to him in all sorts of ways. It is said that when he came from Worksop for his appointment interview in

Canterbury he was sitting in the train and praying quietly for the Almighty's help. He looked out of the window and saw a signpost pointing to 'The King's School'. It was probably indicating The King's School, Grantham, but Shirley took it as a positive sign for himself and had no doubts at all that it was God's will for him to go to Canterbury. He then had the assurance that all would be eventually well and that he was able to take risks at which others would have baulked. And we must remember that for him the school buildings were not the main aim: his interest was not for the school as a place but for the boys in it.

On questions of discipline John Shirley was firm and clear, and the boys appreciated this. An unusual example was when a number of boys one summer had gone out pinching cherries from orchards in the neighbourhood. Suddenly a notice went up on the headmaster's board: 'I understand some boys have been cherry scrumping, and I have a few names. I want to see all involved in my house at two o'clock this afternoon'. This caused a stir: no one knew the names that Shirley possessed. All the offenders, and there were many of them, decided to answer the summons; anyone who had taken cherries dared not stay away for fear of the others' revenge later on. About 50 turned up, saying hopefully to themselves, "Anyway, he can't very well cane the lot of us." Little did they know their man, who started to give them six strokes each, only pausing halfway through to send a note to the Captain of School: 'Come and help, old man. I am nearly exhausted'.

Early on in my time at King's I was told by another member of staff that, if I wanted Shirley's attention when he was busy, it was only necessary to say "Headmaster, I want to see you about a boy", and he would drop everything and give you his undivided attention. One day I used this formula and he immediately put down his pen. "Which one?" he asked. I gave the name. "Ah!" he said, "That's the one who lives in... (he gave his home town) and has the fussy mother." I was always amazed how much he knew about each of his 600 boys and of their backgrounds.

Nothing illustrates better John Shirley's faith and his vocation to his pupils than a letter which he wrote in 1953 to the Lower Master for the staff:

My dear JB,

I wish you would read this and pass it individually to our colleagues to be ultimately returned to you and put on the fire. The subject-matter is mainly religion. There seems to be throughout the school a greater apathy towards religious observances than I can remember, though I do believe that the general character of the place is wholesome and decent...

A conviction of the reality of God and the revelation of Him by our Saviour must, at all events, indicate to us the nature of our tasks as schoolmasters. The schoolmaster, the priest, the doctor alone survived through the dark ages to bring about happier and more civilised times: and in this chaotic and pagan age they seem to me the three principal agencies to make men more what they should be and produce a better world... It is not humbug then if I write that we schoolmasters are God's servants, and if we are Christians in belief and in hope then each of our pupils is a child of God, one for whom as for us Christ died, and for whom we shall be answerable. What a privilege this is and what a responsibility. Nothing separates us from our charges save that we have lived a few more years. We are not more natively clever than some, and we stand in need of God's grace and forgiveness as much as any of them, and probably far more. It has seemed to me for many years therefore that the one right attitude of a master to his boys is that of humility - upon him has fallen by his choice the opportunity of directing his boys to the good life: and therein <u>he</u> will matter; not his brains nor looks, nor athletic prowess - himself.

It follows then that our boys can never properly be regarded in units - just 'this boy', 'that boy'. Each one possesses, nay rather <u>is</u> - his sacred personality, his individual self, unlike every other boy alive; and it is that uniqueness that is really given into our charge to shape and develop...

Now Bruce Wills has left: a charming, utterly good and marvellously brave boy. Fourteen months ago he developed a cancer in the knee; last November the leg was amputated. It is a particular kind of cancer from which recovery is so rare that you might say almost nobody ever does recover. Last term the fateful secondary infection appeared in his chest and back. Two or three of us have known and the medical people have done all that is known in their Science, but there is no hope. The end will come now, it may be in days, or a few weeks - but short of a miracle the doctors pronounce the case hopeless and the end to be soon...*

But it might have been anyone else - the boy with whom we were unduly harsh, the boy we have never thought much of, the dull boy whom it was no pleasure to teach. And a tragedy like this shews how little, <u>in all reality</u>, separates us older ones from our younger Brethren.

Yours sincerely,
John Shirley

Bruce Wills, who had been a member of my house, Meister Omers, died of cancer soon after this letter was written. The truth is that John Shirley thought of everyone as a special child of God, for whom Christ died. He had a great sense of the importance of religion for all of us. He once said, "If it is not true that Christ came to this earth and died for us, then it doesn't matter. But if it is true, then nothing else matters."

* See also page 112

John Dalrymple

John Dalrymple was a chorister and boarder at Canterbury Cathedral Choir School from 1937 to 1940. He was at the King's School, Canterbury, from 1940 to 1944 during its period of evacuation in Cornwall and was Captain of School in the year prior to his leaving to join the Royal Navy. Demobilised in 1947, he went up to Trinity College, Oxford, as a Ford Scholar, graduating in 1950. He joined the Bank of London and South America that year and subsequently served in Argentina, Brazil, Ecuador, Mexico, Venezuela and Spain, retiring in 1986. He was awarded an OBE in 1976. He is currently chairman of the mental health charity, Home in My Mind.

I arrived in Canterbury in 1937 as one of the first 11 boarding members of the Cathedral Choir School. We were the 'outsiders', for up to that time the Cathedral choristers had been drawn from within travelling distance of the city. I do not know whether the radical proposals which changed for the better the Cathedral's music and liturgy had been supported in the Chapter by Canon Shirley, but it would not surprise me to learn that he had opposed them. Although he was not particularly fond of church music (his tastes were operatic and theatrical and he positively disliked early music), he might have resisted any development that would have detracted from the growing reputation of the King's School choir (singing on Sundays in what was sometimes referred to as Shirley's Temple). It was, however, certain that by 1938 relations were strained to breaking point between Shirley and the young and charismatic Choir School headmaster. The result was a barrier to communication between the two schools that lasted throughout my schooldays and was only occasionally breached in spite of the steady stream of choristers who proceeded from the one school to the other.

Canon Shirley stood out from an undistinguished looking Chapter (not counting the magnificently medieval Red Dean, Hewlett Johnson). I did not listen with much attention to his sermons or to the content of the lessons which he read so beautifully, but I was attracted by this figure, ruddy-complexioned, full of life, striding with firm step to the pulpit or lectern. I doubt that he would have spoken to any individual chorister, but I became aware that he had noticed me, probably because my eyes were so often on him.

It happened that I lagged behind my peers in moving from being a mere 'singing boy' to becoming a full chorister. This was because I could not bring myself to sing the required solo in a Cathedral service; the waiting silence terrified me and I had no voice to use. But I had no inhibitions when given the opportunity to act in school plays; and it was a calculated risk that gave me a main singing part in an opera written for boys' voices and performed in the Canterbury Festival of 1939. As a result, and certainly as an exception, I was duly installed as a chorister. This provoked a warm note of congratulation from my favourite Canon, with the promise of a place, subject to my passing the Common Entrance examination, at the King's School.

Before this, there had been some hesitation among my peers about going on to King's because of the headmaster's reputation for beating. Shirley came to hear of this, and the candidates were summoned to 15 The Precincts for a spectacularly good tea laid on by Mrs Shirley. Now one of his most engaging ways was to prod his victim with his forefinger and, depending on whether he was about to censure or not, he would scowl or grin and emit a long and questioning high-pitched "Eeeeee, m'dear....." followed by whatever he had to say. On this occasion the prod-and-grin routine was followed by the statement that choristers, being the angelic creatures that they were, need never fear that this punishment would ever be applied to them. He was of course wildly wrong in this generalisation and most of us knew that he was teasing. But in fact I believe that he never did beat an ex-chorister, certainly in my time, and in spite of provocation.

Thus in 1940 my Canon became my headmaster, and the King's School moved to Cornwall. I fagged for a boy who told me that he had accompanied Fred by car from Canterbury to the school's new quarters at Carlyon Bay, with the headmaster driving most of the way in second gear. Apparently the car never recovered, and in no time Fred had persuaded one of the staff to part with his car so that, in spite of petrol rationing, he could commute in to the school from his country house at Trenarren.

Removal at times from the Carlyon Bay scene did not appreciably lessen his control of the school where order was maintained by his able deputy, 'J B' Harris. Fred had that uncanny knack of knowing in great detail what was going on. This was not so much dependent on a spy network as to his putting the telling question to any boy he might encounter and inferring much from the reply. Some boys, not 'favoured' by him in the sense of preferential treatment of any sort, were nonetheless identified by him as being basically honest and trustworthy in their opinions and judgment. It has been said that some staff felt undermined by this practice, but I suspect that it only really affected those who might have had reason to feel uneasy. Fred could, however, be ruthless with staff, rude and tactless. Sadly, after the last wave of younger masters had left for the Services at the end of the

A Latin class alfresco in the late 1930s. "I found myself in his Latin set for a term - a time of whizzing chalk and flying textbooks interspersed with comment on constipation, colonic irrigation and pustules".

summer of 1940, it was a mixed bag that was left to carry the school through the war, and he sometimes had good reason to despair. The academic achievements were the more remarkable for that.

Not that Fred himself was a particularly good teacher. I fancy he considered that he could coach any boy enough Latin to secure at least an examination pass. I found myself in his Latin set for a term - a time of whizzing chalk and flying textbooks interspersed with comment on constipation, colonic irrigation and pustules. Boys were commanded to report to his study during the break for suitable treatment - not a beating but an appropriate pill. None of us learned much in these lessons, but it was all very exciting with Fred in his prod-and-scowl mode. His was a volcanic and volatile temperament and his anger, though usually short-lived, was something to be feared.

Fred expected sons of the clergy and ex-choristers to be endowed with a special spiritual dimension that they did not always possess. In his dealings with them, as with any boy who showed a genuine interest in religion, he displayed uncharacteristic admiration and humility. It was as though he sensed something in them that he himself lacked. He hoped, indeed expected, that they would submit themselves for ordination, and in this he was often, and inevitably, disappointed. At the end of one term he gave me George Bernanos's *Diary of a Country Priest* as holiday reading and was saddened by my refusal at the beginning of the following term even to consider commitment to the Church. (Disappointed in me, I am glad that he was richly rewarded in the ordination of others.) He had a way of probing religious and moral development that could be disconcerting. He would stand closely in front of you and put his question, first peering intently at your face over the top and then under the bottom of his spectacles. It was impossible to avoid his gaze - and the truth. After one such encounter he sent me packing with the comment, "You're a rum character!" I had no notion of what he meant, though I knew that it was not complimentary. Resort to the dictionary did nothing to enlighten me.

When at the end of the 1943 summer term Fred called me to his study and told me that I was to be the next Captain of School I could scarcely believe my ears. I understand that the wartime Captains of School exercised considerably more authority than their successors. I had been a house prefect for only a term, and I felt overwhelmed by the prospect of such responsibility. But if he had doubts about me as an untried risk, which he must have done, he never expressed them. I always had his unwavering support. This is not to say that our relationship in the year that followed was always on an even keel. I was not so experienced as to be able always to react appropriately to his swings of mood. He could on occasions be childish and even jealous, and negotiation across the ground between headmaster and his staff was a minefield. For a long time after I had left school I never felt so old as I did at 17; but I did acquire some diplomatic skills that were later to stand me in good stead.

During my time as Captain of School I wanted to abolish beating by both headmaster and school monitors, and in this I secured the support, in some cases reluctantly, of the monitorial body. Fred was delighted with our decision but stalled on his part of the pact. Finally he agreed to abstain from caning if we all agreed to admit to him that we had all indulged in those then most heinous of school crimes, drinking beer and smoking, mostly at away matches, with our giving a promise to renounce these pleasures for the rest of our school careers. (I was not popular with those who neither drank nor smoked but who had to admit both.) Whether all on our side kept to the bargain I do not know, but Fred held to his promise, at least as long as I was at the school.

Much has been said and written about Fred's preoccupation with money. This has to be considered in the context of those difficult times and of his own passionate devotion to the school's survival. There was nothing about his lifestyle to suggest that he was personally interested in the acquisition of wealth. He was wont to point out that he did not receive a salary, but he did also say that the school, both directly and indirectly, owed much to the generosity of his wife.

For Mrs Shirley I had the greatest admiration. She was a 'lady'; Fred, for all his Oxford education, his Navy commission, his legal training, his scholarship and his ordination, was not a 'gent'. This had nothing to do with his immediate background, though that may have spurred him on to search for aristocratic antecedents, as the family tree and the coat of arms, displayed for all to see in the hall of Precincts 15, indicated. But there was in him no snob struggling to emerge. Nevertheless he enjoyed the company and, in some cases, the friendship of the good and the great; and he could be extremely charming, particularly when he wanted something - usually for the school.

Throughout his life he kept his good looks. His well-manicured hands were particularly fine. He dressed immaculately, even elegantly; and his shoes were always brilliantly polished. His was the first colourful tie which I remember - red, worn with a grey pin-striped suit.

Fred was the most important influence in my young life, and I owe a tremendous debt to him. Were he alive now I would want to try and repay him for all his care and great kindness to me. In retrospect I think that he was a lonely man. There was no 'side' to him - he always showed 'warts and all'; and although he enjoyed receiving the affection of others, how he was regarded was of no great concern to him. Different boys saw different sides. An OKS once protested to me that Fred was a 'saint'; that would have surprised him. Others, and some staff, did not and do not speak of him well. He was, of course, neither saint nor sinner but a complex, strong and most loveable human being. Dear Fred; how I miss you!

James Peschek

James Peschek went as a music scholar to the King's School, Canterbury, in 1940, having previously been a chorister at All Saints', Margaret Street, and a pupil at its Choir School. He served in the Royal Naval Volunteer Reserve before going in 1946 as a choral scholar to King's College, Cambridge, where he read history and then music. He was Director of Music at Monkton Combe School and then at Uppingham. He retired from full-time teaching in 1985.

Fred was a formidable mentor to whom I owe much. The first of his many acts of kindness to me was when he admitted me to King's, having sat no Common Entrance exam and with my parents hard up. (My voice had broken late, the Choir School had demanded its pound of flesh and I was four months short of my fifteenth birthday when I changed schools.) Perhaps Fred was looking to keep his numbers up or considered that a boy with an Anglo-Catholic background might in some way leaven the lump.

As a new boy I had tea with Fred and his charming wife. I had come to King's with a dread of priestly headmasters, having been beaten somewhat relentlessly at my choir school for trivial misdemeanours. At Canterbury, where the cane was well established, it was nonetheless a blessed relief to find a headmaster who generally appeared to reserve its use for outrageous behaviour (and in my first term I survived, to my surprise, without receiving a single stroke from master or monitor).

Initially we saw little of Fred except in assembly or Cathedral: the phoney war was ending and big decisions were pending as the headmaster, undoubtedly preoccupied with planning and staffwork, tackled the enormous task of efficiently moving the school from one side of England to the other. In that spring of 1940 we returned to Canterbury for a few weeks of the summer term and were then sent home before presenting ourselves at Carlyon Bay Hotel in Cornwall, ready to start school life all over again.

In our new environment Fred had sensibly retained some of the traditional trimmings of uniform, gowns and Canterbury customs. But we had exchanged the Precincts for golden beaches, cliffs, fields and woods, and the Cathedral for the hotel's large garage (which also served as assembly hall, concert hall and theatre). The freedom to explore was new, and the headmaster's forthright notices about the cliffs being out of bounds and his injunctions about smoking in Crinnis Woods tended, I am sorry to admit, to draw attention to their possibilities. There were other problems too: the temporary marriage with St Edmund's (the Clergy Orphan School from Canterbury) which had come to Cornwall with us - different uniforms, different backgrounds, reluctance on the part of many boys to forget that other boarding schools existed only for the purpose of being thrashed on the games field; and there was the King's Junior School (Milner Court) housed across the road in the Bayfordbury Hotel. Fred, the sometimes benign dictator, ruled the school from his first floor study or issued edicts by telephone from his refuge at Trenarren.

One of the big features of our evacuated life in Cornwall was the school drama which Fred always encouraged. It had the advantage of not being a particularly expensive activity, and at any rate in those days the spoken word was more important than complex stage sets and trimmings. On the musical side, Fred's friends, Olive Groves and George Baker, both of whom had sons at King's, came more than once to entertain us with their brilliant singing. Homemade concerts under Dr Henry Phillips were given with a (literally) scratch orchestra, and we had gramophone society recitals, a music club formed for enthusiasts and plenty of choral music (not all of it entirely to Fred's taste).

If Fred's sermons were unmemorable (having heard hundreds at my choir school, I had become adept at enduring them with calm inattention), his special assemblies were a different matter. Here he would rant and rage about our misdeeds and shortcomings or the failure of some of us to wash or to work diligently in sixth form study periods. When he was walking about in the hotel he would prod a particularly dishevelled youth in the stomach with his finger while telling him to present himself in his study with properly cleaned shoes. Also he had an uncanny knack of putting his hand into a boy's jacket pocket and removing from it a packet of cigarettes (20 with luck) prior to administering the cane to the miscreant. Cigarettes were scarce and Fred was always short of them, and he had no compunction in beating the guilty in his smoke-filled study.

He once caned almost the whole of School House for wagering that a house monitor, Ivor Butcher, would not announce the lesson in evening house prayers in the style of a BBC wartime newsreader. Butcher began, "The lesson is taken from [whatever it was] and this is Ivor Butcher reading it." The chaplain had been asked at short notice to take prayers and was not amused. He promptly reported the episode to Fred who stormed down, confiscated the stakes and administered summary justice in his study to all concerned. Butcher, incidentally, got off scot-free and, to my mind, rightly.

One of Fred's *bêtes noires* was the non-Latin set. Convinced that we were idlers - and in some respects he was right - he regularly made us

School Certificate candidates appear in his study after lunch to be questioned on seven different French irregular verbs on each occasion. Hesitant responses or wrong answers were instantly rewarded with one stroke of the cane. I was one in that set blessed with an excellent short-term memory. It saved my bacon but didn't prevent me failing in the summer. His two School Certificate Latin sets seldom escaped lightly. I recall one occasion when halfway through a Latin period in the next classroom his wrath got the better of him. He stormed out roaring, "I won't teach such an idle set of bastards," and strode across the field between the garage-classrooms and the hotel swiping at the thistles and tall grass with his cane as he went. Most of his set passed, but those who failed joined his dreaded endorsement group, filled mainly with boys hoping to read medicine who needed a full 'matric' in order to do so. This set could be something of a blood-bath: there was much roaring and many would have preferred to have eaten their breakfast standing up. Few failed their retake at Christmas. Possibly in spite of this, or because of it, Fred never seemed to have a very high opinion of medicos. One recently qualified Old Boy was greeted on his return with the remark, "Ee, it's a good thing yer don't have to put the mark yer got in yer finals on yer brass plate, m'dear."

With the exception of medical schools, university entry for Fred was a matter of 'Oxbridge or now't'. I and a contemporary set our sights on choral scholarships at King's, Cambridge. Our success in February 1943 delighted Fred who promoted us at once to be school monitors. My housemaster, who had not been consulted on the matter, promptly removed the notice from the school board; he had always regarded musicians as being temperamentally unstable. But, needless to say, the appointments held.

What other memories of this remarkable headmaster? There was the time when my passion for Prokofiev's Classical Symphony caused me to rise early to play the records daily and very loudly in my study. One morning I became aware of some tapping on the window, and there was Fred in full vestments asking me to reduce the volume as he could no longer continue with his communion service "with that row going on". (My apology was accepted.) Then years later, after graduating and just after a tragic suicide in my college, I met Fred again when visiting Canterbury. His memory was remarkable; he wrinkled his nose, gave me the usual stomach prod and said, "Ee, so yer got yer degree in the end, did yer? King's, wasn't it? No wonder the Dean jumped off the roof." The acerbic coda was in character. And some years on, when a chance freedom enabled me to get down to Canterbury for Commemoration, Fred was working hard to get the school boat club re-established. As he was talking to me halfway through tea on the Green Court, he suddenly cut our conversation short with, "Now, old man, there are at least three or four people on this lawn who can afford to give me an 'eight', and before six o'clock I shall have asked them to do so." No doubt he was successful.

Fred had the touch of a genius, and a many-sided one too. He had tried Anglo-Catholicism, socialism and even colonic irrigation! Yet in many ways he was years ahead of his time. Unencumbered with the running of a boarding house, he was the archetypal manager-head possessed of remarkable entrepreneurial skills, confidence and courage, and never afraid to skate on thin ice. Whether or not he really believed that public schools were a good thing, he was determined that King's should be one of the best, and in this he was astonishingly successful. He was quite simply an unforgettable and unique personality and a great headmaster.

Michael Mayne

*The Very Reverend Michael Mayne joined the King's School,
Canterbury, in 1943 during its period of evacuation in Cornwall. He
left in 1949, having been Vice-Captain of School, and after National
Service went to Corpus Christi College, Cambridge, and subsequently
to Cuddesdon Theological College. He was ordained in 1957, and his
various posts since then have included his being Head of Religious
Programmes, BBC Radio, from 1972 to 1979 and Vicar of Great St
Mary's, Cambridge, from 1979 to 1986. In that year he became Dean
of Westminster and retired in 1996.*

My dear John,

for so you always signed yourself and this is the very personal letter
I should have written to you when you were alive. But couldn't. Oh, I
could have expressed a young man's gratitude to one whom I held in a
mixture of awe and affection, and some 40 years ago I tried to do so. A
conventional letter to the most unconventional headmaster in Britain.
But now I am approaching the age you were when you retired from
King's, and I can view you with different eyes and certainly with more
understanding and more compassion; though I recognise how time and
distance quickly distort the reality and that the mind is dangerously
selective.

All of us who contribute to this book will inevitably explore
variations on a common theme: our memory of a man of extraordinary
energy and vision, compassionate, unpredictable, often indiscreet,
whose dynamic commitment to that vision could make him appear at
times to be worldly, even ruthless, yet at other times could reveal the
kindest and most discerning of pastoral hearts. Your vision was of
King's as you eventually made it, of boys enabled to develop their full
potential, and of a society based on Christian values.

If you were ambitious, you were ambitious for the school. If you
knew and weighed the cost of everything, you also knew the worth of
every person, not least boys who were, for one reason or another,
handicapped or in need of friendship and encouragement. Your anger
could be frightening, and you operated on the shortest of fuses. Your
daily intake of nicotine and vitamin pills was impressive. You could be
sullen and peevish and you were easily cast down. You certainly knew
that most of us feared you, made uneasy by the unpredictability of your
moods, but I think you knew that many of us came to love you too. In
the words of your anonymous obituarist in *The Times*: 'His favourite

activity was "getting hold" of a boy with moderate natural gifts, and pouring into him his own liveliness and single-mindedness'. And that's what instinctively drew us to you, pleased that your reputation for eccentricity gave King's a certain cachet, and recognising that you had each individual's deepest interests at heart.

Though you would have been even more remarkable than you were if you had been so even-handed as not to single out certain boys for special attention. I think you did so in my case because my father, a priest, had committed suicide when I was very young, and you took me 'on special terms' (and how many others? A fair number, I guess). By the time you had finished with me my life had been turned in a new direction.

It began in 1948 when you cast me as Hamlet in the first post-war school play in the Chapter House, and directed it with an idiosyncratic brilliance that sometimes left your cast spinning. When we bored you with our lifeless acting at rehearsals you wandered among us, your eyes half-closed, a cigarette hanging from your lower lip, watering the stage with a watering-can; or sat in the back row of that acoustically challenging Chapter House shouting "Can't *hear!*" When Laertes was unconvincing in Ophelia's death scene and the subsequent duel, you cast a second Laertes at a very late stage and divided the part between them ("Under a beard, m'dears, the audience won't know you apart." They did). You bullied us, cossetted us, taught us how to speak Shakespearean verse, and left us exhausted but triumphant. You had shown me my vocation, and I left that term for National Service followed by a life in the theatre. Or so l thought.

I have a sheaf of your letters beside me as I write. The first of them is dated 1949, a fortnight after *Hamlet*, and is ten pages long. It is written on a train journey in an uncharacteristically shaky hand. The nub of it is: 'You think you're going to be an actor. You're not. You're going to be a priest'. And that being so, I was to go to Cambridge. And that meant passing the then compulsory Latin entrance exam. And that meant going back to Canterbury for the whole of June as your guest to have daily Latin sessions with you, often sitting at the foot of your temporary sick-bed, and I didn't dare fail. It was an unlooked-for, typically characteristic, act of kindness.

Your next letter is dated January 1952. You write, spelling out your ideas for establishing a 'King's Week', and ask if I will come in July to play Prince Hal in your conflated version of both parts of *Henry IV*. In the event you conducted the first two rehearsals, got bored, asked me to take over as temporary producer, and indicated that you would then reappear for the dress rehearsal. It still amazes me that I called your bluff and said that either you produced it or I did. So I did. But clearly you were cross and remained remote and offended, and word came back to me of 'the arrogance of undergraduates'. Yet my next letter is a warm and generous letter of apology written late after the opening performance. How absurd it all seems now! But again, how characteristic.

There are other letters that survive, full of news and gossip about King's. One begins, typically:

> Tired as a dog, and only half-awake - just got up late; spent yesterday 8.45 a.m.-9.15 p.m. travelling to and from Southampton to sit with a sick man a few hours, and all the 'connecting' trains ran slow and failed to connect.

In May 1957 I told you that I was to be ordained the following month. If I quote fairly fully from your reply it is because it reads as an apologia for your own priestly life, that deep love of individuals with all their quirky idiosyncracies that motivated you and won the affection of generations of boys, parents and staff.

> Dst. Mike - I am so glad and hope that you have a wonderful life. You will often be vexed and worried - by the recalcitrance of people you want to win - by the curious clergymen you will now and then meet - by the increasing mechanisation of the C of E - by the ambitions and worldliness of too many clerics... and so on. But never, never lose sight of Christ who alone matters; don't let the institutional side of things obscure or distort Him. If our faith means anything it is faith in a Person; not in sets of rules, not in an ethical code, not at all in conventional church respectability; and that Person is God Almighty seen in the Face of Jesus and = Love, which is the originating and sustaining power of all life, and is therefore Eternal, and because Eternal, Love = God. And Love connotes patience and forgiveness and gentleness and sympathy - because in every other we see God if we have eyes of faith and love; of course, because He made us all, He redeemed us all, and gave to each of His professing followers the charge and care of the unlovely and unloving, the ignorant and the difficult. But all this you know - so forgive me - yet I find the Church (so to speak) deficient in love and forgiveness; yet they are the only virtues which will let us take men hand-in-hand and bring them to the Saviour Whom they don't know they need...
>
> I can see you now, vividly, aged fourteen at Carlyon Bay.
>
> Love,
> John Shirley

Most of us are fortunate enough to know one or two unusually gifted, over-lifesized individuals, large personalities who have the power to influence others for good or ill. It shouldn't surprise us that they are as damaged as the rest of us, or that their faults and their vulnerability may be as conspicuous as their talents. You had no illusions about your own flawed humanity. And, though there were times when you struggled to hold together a faith that is intellectually credible and emotionally fulfilling, you never really doubted the centrality of the life, death and resurrection of Christ as the supreme revelation of the love of God for each of us. That is what you helped me to understand, both by preaching it and living it, and that is why I shall never cease to be grateful that, like the best of teachers, you spotted what was in me and gently nurtured it.

With my love,
Michael

Return to Canterbury: King's receives its Royal Charter in 1946. Dean Hewlett Johnson and Archbishop Fisher are on the left. Mrs Shirley and Janet Shirley are to the right of the pillar.

With a parent on Speech Day. " ... new boys, prospective parents or potential staff attending for interview would find themselves listening to what sounded like a confidential revelation of the headmaster's concerns".

Photo: Kent Messenger Group.

Benedict Birnberg

Benedict Birnberg went as a pupil to the King's School, Canterbury, in 1945 and subsequently gained an open scholarship to Corpus Christi College, Cambridge. He was admitted a solicitor in 1958 and is senior partner of B M Birnberg and Co. He has at various times been chairman of the National Council for Civil Liberties, chairman of Lewisham CAB and a governor of Greenwich Theatre Ltd.

I joined the school immediately on its return to Canterbury from Cornwall and my four years were spent as a dayboy. In those days the dayboys were, relatively speaking, a rump, few in number and something of a rag-tag and bobtail, divided between four of the five boarding houses but decidedly peripheral. We were somewhat second class citizens in the vibrant community of boarders who really comprised the school. And so, at least in my first two years, my encounters with the Great Man were relatively few and far between.

In my third year, however, I took a leading part in what we dayboys considered a seditious movement - the organising of a round robin signed by all the dayboys petitioning for the re-establishment of the dayboy house which had existed before the war. Armed with a box of cigars (we had done our homework judiciously) a small delegation presented itself at the headmaster's house at the beginning of the Easter term in 1948 and handed Fred our petition.

Expecting to be slapped down mercilessly, to our surprise and pleasure we found ourselves pushing at an open door. Fred was charm itself. He responded eagerly. We would have our house at the beginning of the Michaelmas term. What should it be called? Marlowe, as it had been pre-war? Or Montgomery? Much as we admired Monty, who was very much the flavour of the month and had visited the school a number of times since the war, we opted for Canterbury's freethinking playwright. And so it came to pass that Marlowe House was re-born, accommodated in the old monastic bakehouse. To cap it all we put on a splendid house concert in the Chapter House that December, featuring amongst other things, a full-length presentation of Marlowe's *Massacre at Paris*, all blood and guts and purple passage, for which we received a congratulatory *billet doux* from Fred.

That portrayed Fred's benevolent self. But there was another side. Although it was said that he owed his appointment in 1935 to the chairman of the governors, Hewlett Johnson, over the years relations with the Deanery had cooled. My years at the school coincided with the onset of the Cold War between the West and the Soviet bloc. Hewlett Johnson, passionate advocate of communism and with his *Socialist Sixth of the World* a bestselling apology for the Soviet Union, was in many respects similar to Shirley, another consummate showman; quite apart from the political divide it was not surprising that they did not always see eye to eye. As curious sixth formers a handful of us were beguiled to attend the occasional agit-prop session in the Deanery, made, I recall, the more palatable by the presence of the opposite sex from Simon Langton Girls' School. Fred's intelligence network was faultless and before long I had one of those fearful summonses. "I have it on good authority that you have been frequenting *that* place" (the adenoidal put-down was unmistakable). "M'dear. If you persist I'll have to beat you" - said with a mixture of sadistic glee and jocular hilarity. My passion for Nowell Johnson's tea and cakes and the Simon Langton brunettes miraculously vanished.*

Fred lived for the school's reputation and, if this meant using its pupils for its greater glory, so be it. As a small example of this, although I had successfully taken my Higher School Certificate examination in my second year in the sixth and got an open scholarship to Cambridge, he arranged for me to be entered for the HSC in the same subjects in my last year simply with a view to improving the school's examination results. In fact I declined to play ball and played truant for much of that last year.

Praise for Fred's superlative skills as an entrepreneur has been sung by so many. That he transformed a small mediocre institution into one of the country's most respected public schools in the four middle decades of this century is now a matter of historical record. Despite his treatise on Hooker (I received three copies of the book as school prizes in consecutive years) he never struck me as essentially an intellectual. His larger than life personality was exactly what the school needed at the time and, looking back dispassionately, I for one consider that his long and unstinted service to the school he loved much outweighed any negative characteristics.

---

* See also page 105

Anthony Curry

The Reverend Anthony Curry was born in 1931 and was a pupil at Canterbury Cathedral Choir School before going in 1945 to the King's School, Canterbury, where in 1949 he was made Captain of School. He subsequently read music at St Edmund Hall, Oxford, and was later ordained, returning to King's in 1956 as Chaplain. He held further posts as Rector of Penshurst, Director of Music at Kelly College and Rector of Brasted before retiring to Burgundy in 1993 where he continues work as a music examiner and organ recitalist.

I joined King's in September 1945 and, having been allocated a place in the Shells, I felt after the first week or so that the work I was being given was rather simple. I made enquiries of my housemaster whether I could be put into a higher form. "You had better go and see the headmaster," came the reply. In break a queue of boys would await their turn along the passage outside the head's study and down the staircase which led up to it. When my time came I put my case and was told that I had better go into the fifth form and see if I could keep up. It turned out to be a comparatively simple procedure: I just explained to my Shell teachers, "The headmaster said...," and then to each fifth form teacher repeated the same formula. No eyebrow was raised! I had learned, without meaning to, that the head was flexible in dealing with pupils of the school as individuals, that his decisions were prompt (if, I later found out, sometimes impulsive) and that the staff were used to, and appeared happily to accept, such decisions being taken without their being consulted or even informed by him. When some years later I joined the staff myself it was an observation to bear in mind!

One year later I again went to see him to ask if I could 'skip' the lower sixth year and go straight into the upper sixth. This time he agreed more reluctantly, coming up with a bargain that I could do as I requested provided that I went on a *satisfecit* (a daily report on one's work which had to be shown in person to the headmaster every 24 hours). A doubtful comment about English literature was noted quite early on and produced the injunction to learn the first act of *Hamlet* and return in three days' time prepared to recite it to him. It was during this period that I first began to feel that I knew and liked him. Often the *satisfecit* was not actually looked at. Instead he would talk about the school and his hopes and plans for it, sometimes as though he were a general planning a strategy, sometimes as though he were a mother talking about her family. The varying moods were as interesting as the proposals themselves. I never recall his dismissing me from his presence by word of mouth - it was usually a gesture, a grunt or a look, and one knew that there was no more he wished to say on that occasion.

His habit of communicating with both boys and staff by means of open cards (sometimes written in a sort of shorthand, or even deliberately enigmatic so that the individual bearer of the missive would be unaware of its portent) was legendary. In the 1949 summer term I received just such a card with the message, 'Haven't seen you for a long time'; so I duly presented myself at 15 The Precincts. The conversation ranged through his usual sequence of priorities: the good of the school; the difficulties of persuading the Dean and Chapter that one of the great opportunities, if not the principal purpose of the Cathedral and its Precincts, was to help him bring up a whole new generation of schoolboys inspired by the Christian faith and dedicated to its ideals of using talent and advantage in the service of others; then the personal and individual bit - the next step, as he envisaged it, for the individual boy he was addressing. It transpired on this occasion that there was really nobody suitable to be Captain of School the following year and, now that 'push' was becoming 'shove', he wanted me to stay on at school an extra year and see if I could make a fist of the job.

I pointed out that I already had a place awaiting me at St Edmund Hall for October and I wondered whether it would be possible to unravel that agreement. I also said that my parents, who had made great sacrifices to send me to King's in the first place, could certainly not afford another year's school fees. His immediate response was to undertake to write to Oxford and arrange for a postponement of my place there and himself to arrange payment of my school fees for the following year. I returned to my house, asked the opinion of my housemaster and took his advice to accept the offer. The significant change for me was that I now knew, when talking to the head, that he was noting what I said as well as wanting me to take note of what he said - that had not previously been obvious to me.

During this last year at school I was often in daily touch with him (though it did take me a week or two to learn that this was really a requirement made of the head boy). We would talk a great deal about religion and theology and I was frequently lent books on these subjects which he had found inspiring or challenging. When I went up to Oxford my vocation to the priesthood became much clearer. I had been writing to him every couple of months or so and always received a prompt and wide-ranging reply. I now wrote to tell him of this development. He promptly asked me to go and stay with him and Mrs Shirley in their home during the next vacation. On my visit we talked late into the night: the distinction between being a Christian and being a priest of the Church of England, the snares of hypocrisy, the difficulties about being part of the Establishment in the eyes of one's parishioners while also being the guardian of one's own conscience. I eventually retired to bed after a stimulating evening and soon fell asleep. Sometime later he came into the room without putting on the light (the open doorway was light enough), came to the head of my bed and gave me a formal blessing. He then traced a baptismal cross on my forehead and quietly went out again. I have never known to this day whether he knew that I was actually awake at the time. It remains with me a vivid memory. Several of my contemporaries at King's were later to be ordained, and I fully expect that, as in my own case, the influences of many priests, lay people, books, experiences and events share responsibility for forming the sense of vocation. I am sure that I am not alone in having been first pointed in that specific direction by Fred.

After Oxford and Wells Theological College I became a curate in the Rochester diocese but, within a few months of my appointment, had the misfortune to be deprived of a visionary priest as vicar of the parish when he went to be Rector of Penshurst. Being single-handed in a parish as but a deacon presented problems and the Bishop of Rochester suggested that I should be on the look-out for another post as soon as the parish's future was assured by the appointment of a new incumbent. It was soon afterwards that I received one of Fred's cards bearing the message, 'Dear A.B.C., Would you like to be chaplain here? Love, F.J.S'. I wrote back in similar format, 'Dear F.J.S., Yes, please. Love, Tony'. So it was that I became chaplain to the school which I had left six years earlier. I saw much of the headmaster but the actual 'deal' struck between us was that I should be paid not as a teacher but as a curate (with the concomitant arguments which I had so often heard before that the school was in financial straits - "We're not endowed like Winchester, m'dear" and "I do this job for nothing, m'dear" - and anyway I felt very much indebted to him for his help in financing my last year as a boy).

With marriage and two daughters family finances soon became strained. So it was that I took a holiday job as a Canterbury taxi driver. We had radio-controlled cabs and one day I was called up on my radio to accept a fare from 15 The Precincts. The receptionist, knowing my address was very close, wondered whether I might not be embarrassed and offered to send another cab instead. I agreed to take the job and drove straight up to the front gate of Number 15 and rang the bell at the threshold I had so often crossed in different circumstances. FJS came to the door and was momentarily nonplussed. He was carrying a small attaché case which I took from him to put in the luggage bay (it was an ex-London cab). I held the door open for him and asked, "Where to, please, Sir?" "East station," came the succinct reply, and we set off. At the station I held the door open for him, carried the attaché case to the doorway leading onto the platform and asked for the fare. It was promptly paid; but holding my hand out a fraction longer than necessary, as is a taxi driver's wont, I was given a poke in the ribs and a mischievous grin. I think that this was the only occasion when I felt he was slightly at a loss for words but his sense of humour did not fail him!

Late in 1960 he told me of his intention to retire from the headship in 1962. At the time I did not believe that, once having made such a, for him, momentous decision, he would be able to bear going on for another 18 months - in my experience he had so often acted spontaneously. I therefore resolved to make my own departure coincide with his (I was apprehensive at continuing in the same position under new leadership) and thought the right moment for going would be in July 1961. I was quite wrong. He retired as head in July 1962 as he had planned and I never heard that the school showed any sign of *rallentando* during that final year. In the case of one who was so imaginative, with such wide horizons - despite such a devoted and long-lasting commitment to one purpose - that final year spoke volumes for his own vocational sincerity.

Roy Purnell

Roy Purnell was an Open Scholar of Jesus College, Oxford. He joined the staff of the King's School, Canterbury, in 1945 and became its head of English. He retired in 1969 and died in 1996.

In 1945, during his last months in Cornwall, Canon Shirley, I was later told, surveyed his ageing teaching staff assembled one day for morning prayers and remarked, "We need some new faces here." I was to be one of those, and my application for the post of senior classics master brought me an invitation to come and see him.

Apprehensive at the prospect of facing one who combined legal and priestly qualifications with the experience of two headships, I quickly found that I was confronting a charming and affable gentleman who, instead of examining my paper claims and enquiring about the omissions, talked with the utmost freedom about the inadequacies of his present staff and his plans for the future. As I listened I became the more eager to join him and help implement what he had in mind, believing that I could surely do much better than those whose weaknesses he had so graphically described.

During the course of this interview there were two interruptions which stand out clearly in my memory after the passage of some 50 years and which, in retrospect, told me something of the man. The first was when Miss Milward, his faithful secretary, came in and informed him that he would not be able to have the use of his car later in the day because Mrs Shirley needed it. He protested and was again told that his wife required it. That too failed to satisfy him and the argument went on in front of me for some minutes with the dispute unresolved. He was acting like the spoilt little boy who, if he made a fuss, would get his own way from the governess. The second interruption came when Janet, his clever and attractive daughter, burst into the room holding a book of Latin unseens. She explained that she could not understand one of the poems, and her admiring father said, "Can't you, m'dear? It's lucky that we have the very man to help you. Mr Purnell knows all there is to know about Latin." The book was handed to me and I scanned the poem by Martial, a writer not usually studied in schools. I translated the piece, having to make a stab at the meaning of one key word which I had never met before (my *Lewis and Short*, referred to later, confirmed my guess). Was this test of my knowledge a preconceived stratagem between father and daughter, or was it an unplanned opportunity, brilliantly seized and exploited by Shirley? I do not know.

I have various memories of the start of my Canterbury career. My appointment was speedily followed by the offer of a Precincts property, for which I was extremely grateful. Some six years later, however, I received from the school solicitor notice to relinquish the tenancy; Shirley wished to trade in my dwelling to secure from the Dean and Chapter larger premises for a day house. Was a solicitor's letter the pleasantest way of giving me this news?

Before the beginning of my first term I went to consult Shirley about my duties and the details of examination set books. I had scarcely launched into my list of questions when he told me that there were "three young gentlemen" seeking Oxbridge entry in English and that I was to be their instructor. This alarming piece of news was to usher me into my position as head of English. Also, during this initial term he sent me various cards: one invited me to take charge of the school library; another bequeathed me care of the textbook store; I was then required to oversee the school magazine; and my last order was to coach English to his daughter, Janet. And of course in addition to all this I had my classes in English literature to be taught to the highest level and, despite considering myself fairly well read, I had never before aspired to teaching the subject. The thing was that for Shirley the word 'impossible' did not exist; anyone using it to him would be awarded a dig in the ribs and an uncertain future.

In these early days after the war Shirley was seeking to enhance the school's academic achievement, and this led him into appointing staff with Oxbridge firsts and doctorates in the hope that these qualifications would guarantee the pupils' success. It was not necessarily a wise policy and big mistakes were consequently made. There was the man who had done brilliantly in the Civil Service examinations but whose voice in class was the only one not to be heard; and there was the Cambridge prizeman who, although interesting and instructive to adults, talked far above his students' heads. Then there was a most serious lapse of judgment on Shirley's part when a cleric, armed with a D Phil, a first in modern languages and the ability to play a Beethoven sonata perfectly, was appointed on four separate occasions, leaving three times during Shirley's regime and once in his successor's. This unfortunate man's failure to control a class was only the most obvious of his defects, and the kindest motive for so many re-engagements must have been Shirley's sense of pity for a misfit. Gifted and successful in so many ways, he nevertheless made his mistakes.

Shirley also had some notable successes in bringing onto his staff young men who came to play a good part in the classroom, on the field and as housemasters. One of these decided to seek a headship. He was not immediately successful and Shirley, conscious that the man's department had already quite enough masters, decided to help him by coaching him in the questions and answers to be expected at interview before governors. The man was a conscientious pupil but still continued to fail in securing promotion. Ultimately Shirley cried out, "Now we'll go through it all again. Only this time don't look as if you're having an attack of diarrhoea." The headship was gained.

In my early King's days as head of English I was much troubled by the lack of qualified assistance to help me with the big increase of sixth form students in the subject. Shirley heeded my worries and made two very good appointments. The first owed less to the quality of his English degree and more to his expertise as an oarsman and musician (both areas of the school which Shirley was trying to develop). The other, an Oxford college organist, not only taught full-time English, played for school services and coached athletics; to these responsibilities were soon added the posts of bursar and housemaster, and this meteoric rise was followed by an equally rapid fall - and a teaching post swiftly secured in the Antipodes.

Shirley's relations with his staff were variable; new masters seemed often to wear haloes that tended to fade quickly. And there was his reluctance in the immediate post-war years to keep our salaries in line with those paid at similar schools. There was no settled scale of remuneration, and the raising of this issue in private or at a masters' meeting was sure to excite his displeasure. He made no secret of the fact that, at least for some time, he took no salary from the school; but he was reticent about his Canon's stipend and his other sources of income. He once informed me that the value of his possessions would probably not reach three figures!

As a public speaker Shirley did not attempt a polished classical style but, more importantly, could powerfully make his appeal to the feelings of his audience. He so tightly held the attention of his listeners that they could not but applaud; and when he claimed, quite unashamedly, that he knew nothing about education, the Speech Day gathering of parents greeted his remark with considerable enthusiasm. He could similarly appeal to a congregation. I recall, when one evening he was preaching to the school in the Eastern Crypt, how skilfully he paused after a more than usually impassioned passage and then, leaning over the pulpit, softly began again, "And then, m'dears..." The fact was that he was a good actor, and his sermons seemed to come from the heart, as perhaps they did.

Before the smaller audience of a masters' meeting he appeared less at ease. When, for instance, he entered the room clutching a bottle of smelling salts, we could not refrain from wondering how he regarded us. And when he prefaced his complaints and admonitions with a prayer, we would ponder whether he was inviting the Almighty to aid him in the face of possible opposition. More dangerous was the advice he once gave when a large number of young and inexperienced men joined our ranks. They were bidden when meeting their first classes to "take the largest youth and hit him hard". I trust that they adopted the spirit of the injunction rather than its literal application.

As a disciplinarian he had one great gift, a nose for the detection of mischief or ill-doing: an unexpected descent upon a study or common room frequently revealed what he had come to find. Also he would sometimes show a closer acquaintance with the boys' activities than did their housemasters. At one masters' meeting, for example, he waxed eloquent over the subject of 'wenching' and ended by citing the recent case of a senior boy who, but for his intervention, might well have been forced to marry a 'town' girl. A housemaster, sitting at the long table opposite the Master of Studies and me, whispered, "Whose house?" Back from my colleague came the crushing reply, "Yours."

His many duties severely restricted Shirley's appearances in the classroom. Strangely the subjects he chose to teach were not the history or divinity for which his qualifications would have recommended him. Once he took a junior form through *Macbeth*, himself playing all the parts, and he would sometimes say, "Anyone can teach English." If his teaching of Latin is to be judged by the tiny booklet of Latin constructions which he issued, it would not be acceptable today. As an Edwardian he perhaps laid too much reliance on Latin grammar and Kennedy's primer, a method likely to alienate the student. When in the late '40s he found the Latin School Certificate results disappointing, he insisted on doubling the time spent on the subject for the following year's examinees; I hope that the results pleased him, but the chief effect of his treatment of the language, already in some quarters diagnosed as dying, was to kill interest in it stone-dead for most of the pupils.

Shirley's energy in pursuit of the school's advancement was unflagging, and his identification with it was so close that the mention to an outsider of either 'King's Canterbury' or 'Canon Shirley' would immediately evoke the response of the other name. He would recharge his batteries by walking or retirement to bed, and these two avocations left him time to brood over his employees and to suspect that they were taking the opportunity afforded by his absence to relax their efforts. This feeling would sometimes be communicated to individuals by the appearance in pigeon-holes of a short critical note or to the staff in general by a letter to the Lower Master which was then circulated from master to master as if it were nothing less than a state secret.

In sum, he was a man of many gifts, of changing moods and of much charm. He used all these attributes to win for himself and his school the recognition which his position as a Canon of Canterbury could only partially provide. He was a most interesting character and, of this I am sure, a great headmaster.

Richard Roberts

Richard Roberts was a pupil at the King's School, Canterbury, from 1945 to 1951 and was Captain of School in his final year. During his subsequent National Service he was commissioned into the Royal Artillery. He then went on to Jesus College, Cambridge. In 1956 he returned to King's as a member of its teaching staff, becoming both a housemaster and head of modern languages. He was later headmaster of Wycliffe College and then of King Edward's School, Witley.

Of course we all *spoke* of him as 'Fred', but I have retained to this day a selection of those characteristic cards with the heading 'From the Headmaster', nearly all hand-written, arriving with a top corner turned down and all signed 'F.J.S.' I also kept a few letters, some short and business-like, even cryptic, others much longer, almost confessional in their readiness to share his current preoccupations. With one exception these are all signed with the three initials - and this is how I prefer to think of him. The exception is important: a letter to which he attached particular weight bears the signature 'John Shirley'. 'John' is how his wife referred to him as did friends of his own age who had not been pupils or staff, a significant reminder that there were aspects of his life which were not wholly dominated by the schools to which so much of it was devoted.

The initials also indicate the complexity, the enigmatic quality of the man. The majority of the cards and letters in my possession were written in 1950/51, when I was Captain of School, or just after I had left, exchanging the privacy of my study in School House for an army barrack-room where they arrived as from another planet. A few more date from the six years after my return to King's in 1956 as a master and his retirement in 1962. The former period was definitely the closer relationship and yet I was never sure then, and am scarcely any wiser now, as to the real essence of his personality. Perhaps this was the secret of the fascination, the 'magus' quality which he exerted.

My earlier impressions as a junior boy were those of a distant but dynamic presence, the smartly-dressed, formally-gowned figure at Morning Prayers, or of him striding down to Birley's for a 1st XV match, with his rakish broad-brimmed hat, long white tie instead of clerical collar, and twirling his stick. There was a touch of the dandy about him; he set store by good tailoring and, above all, by the quality of footwear. But he was not aloof: new boys enjoyed the tea-parties at Number 15 where Mrs Shirley presided with kindly serenity while he roamed about picking up useful scraps of school gossip, once we had relaxed and after he had helped us to do so. Meeting him casually about the Precincts one was not ignored; he might well pause with a twinkling eye to remind himself of your identity, and he had cultivated the skill of storing names and background details to an impressive and useful extent.

His 'persona' somehow exerted a powerful influence even in his absences, which were frequent. There were governors' meetings and visits to London, Oxford or, more rarely, Cambridge; there were his regular Thursday outings, often day-long walks. Just once, aged 19, I accompanied my 60-year old headmaster on foot from Canterbury to Stodmarsh, on to Plucks Gutter and northwards to Herne Bay, where I was much relieved that he was willing to board a bus home. There were also weeks at a time when he took to his bed with some mysterious ailment, often receiving visitors in his bedroom and, if he needed cigarettes, dispatching senior boys to buy them. It was suggested that these maladies often coincided with his scheduled months as Canon-in-Residence. More than once, in the depths of the Easter term, he needed several weeks to recuperate in the south of France. In my last year, on his well-advertised birthday, we presented him with a (one way) ticket to Nice which was readily subscribed.

Whether he was physically present in Canterbury or not, he had created a set-up which continued to function effectively. We might guess that he was away because the stalwart, phlegmatic J B Harris presided at Prayers in his stead. But there was always an element of uncertainty: he might reappear unheralded, sometimes with unerring instinct at the most awkward time or place, such as a sixth form study during an idle 'free period'. The headmaster's noticeboard was also a projection of his authority. Occasionally it published an execution - 'Jones. Smoking. 6', or, after Fortnightly Orders, the list of those on *satisfecit* required to show daily evidence of better work, or other names bracketed with the ominous 'See me. F.J.S.'

He was undoubtedly an energetic man, despite those apparently lethargic spells in bed, but he directed his energies primarily to strategic tasks: the formulation of plans and policies, followed by their persuasive communication and propagation through long letters and private interviews. Above all he was concerned to promote the school - and he was brilliant at it. He did not find much time for teaching, certainly at least when I knew him, on any regular basis. All the normal school work, particularly at the top of the school, and much of its planning, was left to those key staff, particularly heads of department to whom, usually but not invariably, he entrusted the main direction of academic matters.

If, however, he was dissatisfied, he would infiltrate a younger man whom he considered more promising - or malleable - in a manner which could undermine and probably demoralise the senior person. Occasionally he would take over some hapless lower Latin class for a ferocious few days' intervention backed by a volley of disproportionate 'learning preps' and the threat of draconian tests of verbs and vocabulary. Whether these were actually followed up, or resulted in the punishments which were firmly believed to be the result of failure, I am inclined to doubt. The apprehension that he might intervene was the important factor for boys and staff alike.

It would be wrong, however, to think that he was not concerned with details of discipline and administration. A note to me is a good example:

To the Captain of School.
I see that on Tuesday last at 11.30 p.m. one young gentleman from Grange and one from M.O. returned. Know who? F.J.S.

Or here is another:

When next you talk to the school do remind them that one of the principal Hallmarks of a gentleman are clean and tended <u>nails</u>! (Some are shockingly filthy.) Continue that cleanliness is not only Christian and anyhow 'next to godliness' but traditionally a feature of the Public School Class - as exemplified in the swell and expensive schools where (as at Winchester etc.) the <u>morning cold bath</u> is de rigueur. Next that the Grange may exempt itself from tradition and good manners in this way but it is the part of other Houses to be kind to them by the encouragement of washed example.
Lastly that <u>shoes</u> (quality and cleanliness) are another Hallmark, as are collars and Brushed Clothes. F.J.S.

The cleanliness of shoes and general sartorial elegance, or the lack of it, were issues on which he chided me personally more than once, both as boy and man. Visiting his home one evening in that last year of my schoolboy career I was ushered upstairs to find him in bed, but cheerful. Glancing down he noticed that my shoes were down-at-heel and unpolished. (He wore the most beautiful, gleaming hand-made shoes himself, which he spent much time cleaning for relaxation and therapy.)
"What size do you wear, m'dear?"
"Seven, sir," I confessed, with embarrassment.
"So do I. Look in that cupboard."

I went over to the cupboard and disclosed several rows of shining footwear.

"Choose a pair, old man."

I picked out the finest brogues I have ever owned and wore them for years to come. I was careful to give them a rub before other visits to Number 15.

He also took the trouble to follow up hints of problems or difficulty for individual boys. Two examples will suffice:

Please see me about -----: important. F.J.S.
Have a look at -----: rum mood they tell me. F.J.S.

Although I have indicated that he could give an impression of remoteness, he was in fact extraordinarily approachable as a headmaster. It was never necessary to have an appointment to see him, though in a crowded break-time outside his study you might be advised by his secretary, the indomitable Miss Milward, to try again at such and such a time. After lunch he usually returned to Number 15 where his accessibility was one of his most attractive and impressive characteristics. The outer door stood open until late in the evening; there was no need to ring. Any boy was welcome to go straight into the hall and knock on the second door on the right, his study. Normally FJS was to be found there at his desk, writing. I never found him impatient or unwilling to be disturbed. "What do you want, old man?" Or very occasionally, "Just a minute, m'dear. Go in next door and talk to my wife while I finish this." (Mrs Shirley's presence, it should be said, was a reassuringly normal and, I should guess, enormously stabilising, supportive influence in his life. She never gave the impression of fluster, upset or embarrassment despite his unpredictable changes of mood or his tendency to an outrageous or provocative remark.)

Any conversation with FJS was likely to be conducted on his terms. Thus new boys, prospective parents or potential staff attending for interview would find themselves listening to what sounded to them like a confidential revelation of the headmaster's concerns. His hopes, plans and frustrations would be revealed to whoever was available. Sometimes they left without really mentioning the purpose of their visit, or wondering how the headmaster had formed any view of them at all. Those encountering this for the first time often felt a sense of privileged insight into his mind; this was part of FJS's fascination. Others who later discovered that they had been the subject of comment - members of staff out of favour, for instance - reacted very differently, with dismay or outrage.

He spent many hours committing his thoughts to paper in his clear, tidy, flowing, yet very legible hand. Here again the recipient was likely to feel that he was invited to share, and support, the plans, policies and hopes that he poured out. The letter which follows, written to me in the autumn term of my year as Captain of School, is a good example of his style and of the sense of partnership with the senior boys which he often articulated and largely achieved. It also contains many of his favourite themes and represents a summary of his aims, and to a great extent the achievements, of the last decade of his headmastership. Its full quotation needs no apology.

27 Nov. 1950

Dear Richard - I talk to the School or some part of it so often that my influence can hardly be other than lessened. Yet I do long to put to the older boarders, say all Sixth Forms and those over 17, the question of the status of the School and its development. This matters to and affects the boys in ways in which it cannot touch me. As I have said before, when I resign I have finished - not in my affection, but in my power to help. If you yourself were to place the whole of this matter before the boys I think it would be more helpful than anything.

At the present moment the School is well thought of, and deserves to be, for the results in all spheres which it attains and for the wholesome character it possesses. But - in our privacy and honest opinion - we cannot pretend it is in the front rank of the Public Schools in common everyday understanding. Westminster, which is the nearest parallel to us, is so, and we are not. We have certainly come up a great deal, because 15 years ago we were only one of many King's Schools. But are we to stop on this rung of the ladder to which we have climbed? You and your contemporaries cannot wish that, partly for the very love you bear the place, and partly because in after-life you want to be proud of the School's place in the public esteem. Now the present boys alone can for the most part ensure this lawful ambition. Those of us who are not in that sense members of the School can assist, but not bring about.

What then are the factors that would ensure success?

First, there must grow a tradition that boys stay a long time, an average of 5 years. This is in a boy's hands, for no parent likes to go against his son's desires, and loyalty to the school calls forth pride and satisfaction in any father's heart.

Second, we must have a scholarly Sixth, which we can come to if boys are here long enough, and if they keep in contact with their Preparatory Schools and help to recruit the better sort.

Thirdly, every boy who wins a Scholarship or Exhibition to Oxford or Cambridge does a splendid job for the School as well as himself.

Then, it is necessary that boys shall take the best degrees at the University that they can; thereby begetting in the minds of the colleges that Canterbury boys are among the very best.

Next, it is essential that the School's character shall be known as sound, happy and wholesome; this again is within the power of the boys and of nobody else. If they wished, bad language, obscenity, sexual misbehaviour, bullying, dishonesty, could disappear overnight.

Then, it is most necessary that we shall improve our Fixture lists. This is not much within the province of the boys, but I assure that everything that can be done is being done. In this context, therefore, you will see the supreme importance of the development of the Boat Club, and the emergence of the School into 'Eights'. Socially our Rowing Fixture List is the best and Eights will only increase its standard. This may well lead to fixtures in other games with Schools of the front rank.

Finally, the Preparatory Schools from which we draw are mixed in quality and standing. Some are first-grade, some not very good. The members of the School who come from the better class of Preparatory Schools can do far more than they know as ambassadors, and they need no counsel as to what should be done.

We hope to open St Martin's House in May, and I feel sure that we shall have the co-operation of all in making the new House - the last there will ever be - a very great success.

If you would like to talk to the boys on all this fore-going material and even read this letter to them I shall be very happy.

Yours ever,

John Shirley

I remember finding this letter persuasive and wishing to do my best to support the aims expressed. It strikes me still as sincere and realistic. Much came to fruition in the next decade, or laid the foundations for further progress under his successors. There is, for me, special interest in the short paragraph dealing with imponderables, that 'wholesome' character in which the uglier features of boarding school life might be minimised. I believe that he was more successful than many headmasters of his time in reducing or controlling problems of this kind. His direct appeal to the boys themselves, often repeated in assemblies or in connection with some particular incident, did have its moral effect; and, as I have suggested, the force of his personality, creating a degree of apprehension, strengthened by the unpredictability of his reactions, acted as a deterrent to wrongdoing. His anger could be fierce but was not irrational. He was capable of unusual tolerance and understanding, especially towards those who went to him in confidence. I did this once myself together with a contemporary. He listened to us without interruption or censure, gave us sensible, practical advice, treated the matter with complete discretion and never referred to it again.

On the other hand there was a moment in my last summer term when I experienced the full sense of FJS's disapproval. The School IV in which I was rowing had been summarily and unexpectedly knocked out of the very first round of the Public Schools event at Marlow Regatta in a Friday evening heat; worse still we had lost to Tonbridge despite beating them earlier in the season.

We offset our own disappointment by staying on at the regatta through the Saturday (except for one righteous soul who returned to Canterbury straightaway on his own). As Captain of Boats I could certainly have influenced our decision although, in retrospect, I thought the master in charge might have insisted otherwise instead of leaving it to us. Lunch-time at the High Table on Monday, where it was my lot to sit next to the headmaster, passed in a distinctly sultry silence. Tuesday was no better but nothing specific was said. In the end I decided to call on FJS and clear the air. I put his reaction down mainly to his own probable disappointment at our failure to win; so, finding him alone in his study, I launched into an apology along those lines. Not at all; he replied that it was the lack of responsibility and leadership on my part which mattered. Taken aback I suggested - not altogether seriously - that he might in that case resolve the matter by swift punishment. Thus I received, in my last term and not far from my twentieth birthday, the only corporal punishment I ever experienced. It was laid on pretty lightly; FJS gave the matter no publicity, nor did I; and relations returned immediately to normal.

In considering this bizarre incident it is worth saying that the discipline he exerted did not rely primarily on corporal punishment but much more on force of personality. He used the cane, I would guess, no more frequently and probably less than most headmasters of his time. He permitted its use by staff and by school monitors, but their recourse to it in my time at school was rare. If it had been more regular or excessive I suspect he would have intervened. Expulsions were rare too; no doubt he eschewed bad publicity; but he also preferred to correct and reform; he may well have had an instinctive sympathy for the rebel or the more independent personality. There were certainly boys who stayed at school despite serious misdemeanours on their part.

During the post-war years the somewhat ludicrous hierarchy of 'privileges' and dress codes was gradually eroded. FJS let this happen naturally and certainly did not resist the process. Bullying was rare and in no way systematic. The introduction of a tutorial system not only sharpened up academic supervision but strengthened a genuine interest in what in later years came to be called 'pastoral care'. But FJS already expected this of his staff, his housemasters in particular, and the monitors. It stemmed naturally from his own interest in boys as individuals. In this respect he was, I believe, ahead of his time, deserving of the loyalty and affection of many boys and their parents towards him.

The picture of FJS seated at his desk writing letters or messages is a typical memory. He communicated best either one-to-one or in front of an audience, preaching a sermon, addressing an assembly, or on Speech Day. I do not remember any staff meetings. Debate and discussion were not his style, although he did summon the school monitors or heads of houses from time to time to talk about problems of discipline or his vision of the school's future and how we might help to bring that about.

Several of the main themes of that vision are echoed in the cards or shorter notes which he sent me as my last school year wore on. It seems to me now that he was using me as a kind of ADC or junior PA. I had very little academic commitment during what was for me a final extra year as Captain of School, but I was receiving an education in a certain style of administration and man-management. Another note from him:

1. Cantuarian
2. Job
3. Meeting. F.J.S.

He allowed me to do most of the routine editorial work on *The Cantuarian* [the school magazine], in itself useful training. I have no idea what the 'Job' might have been. The 'Meeting' would have been for head boys of the boarding houses. The agenda for it was contained in another note:

1. Discipline
2. Morals
3. Entry & Leavers
4. Any other business

I suggest that after these [entry] Schol. exams are over, I'd like you and Stephen [Young] to show the Schol. boys round a bit - when they see how nice you are, they'll all want to come.

F.J.S.

A longer note refers yet again to the leaving list in detail, with names arranged by houses with question marks in several cases:

The likely people leaving in July, apart from those who (a) must and those who (b) contribute little are...

Better tactics might be for each Head to talk to all the 17 year olds and

over as to the needs of the School and their own part - for none would
suffer by remaining... I feel after July we may write up 'Ichabod' over
the gates... a young Sixth, an exam-grab attitude of education, a fragile
XV, a hockey XI defeated by Ramsgate etc!!! F.J.S.

Meetings with senior boys were of course easy for him to dominate.
I wonder now about governors' meetings, but there too, I dare say, he
was ready to give a performance (there is a revealing glimpse in a later
letter to be quoted in its context). His lines of communication ran more
easily through older boys and some younger staff with whom he had
warmer relationships. There were also older men (one thinks of the two
Harrises, J B and R W, or J H Corner at one period) on whom much
devolved. Some parents too, I believe, were treated as friends and
confidants.

He was capable of writing at great length, and amusingly, perhaps
partly for relaxation or to clear his own mind. An example is a letter
written to me during the autumn of 1951 when I was starting National
Service at Oswestry. Some of it was, as he put it, 'gossip' and 'private
as to some obvious and uncharitable things' - he knew his own faults!
His comments on academic priorities and the place of the Corps are
revealing, but he is above all anxiously awaiting the results of a school
rugby match:

> ...the odd times of today [a Saturday] may not exhaust all the drivel, or I
> may easily dry up but postpone fastening the letter till the news of the
> Eastbourne match arrives tonight - if it does... Term has started, it seems,
> not too badly in general ways. The work side presented a more serious
> problem than usual, because of the unexpected results of the new
> examinations, the necessity of creating at once two additional Forms
> between the Shells and Fifths, the number of successful examinees who
> did not want to do what I wanted them to do, and the number of
> unsuccessful ones who desired to take the examinations in December,
> contrary to my wishes. Most of all this has been sorted out and the
> Russian work has begun, and is proving not unpopular.
>
> A larger number of Upper School boys than usual desire to resign
> from the Corps and one has presented me with his manifesto thereon. It
> is well-written, cogent and unanswerable; but I can't let him go! I feel
> keenly for them and wish we hadn't one, but we have, & it is part of the
> Public School set-up... and its repercussions are important. If we
> abolished it, all the old men sitting in armchairs in the clubs of Pall Mall
> and St. James would redden with vexation, attribute it to the Dean, and
> gossip that the King's School must be a hot-bed of young reds and
> conchies. It is a difficult puzzle, and I don't know the answer... So I must
> just shoo the poor boys off, as best and comfortably as I can...

The letter then continues with an analysis of the 1st XV's opening match against Canterbury RFC, a narrow win, and a débâcle against KCS Wimbledon, unfortunately reported by the *Times* correspondent:

...So on Monday night I asked for a meeting with Meadows [in charge of rugby] and the Chaplain [John Edmunds, who assisted]... now a quantity of new boys have arrived for tea, so that I am compelled to break off, and renew as soon as I can decently leave this young society... I have now returned to my charming study with some uncertainty as to my next movements. For at tea I learned from the free chatter of the young that for the last night or two 'political' meetings have been held amid riotous behaviour and the throwing of tomatoes and other missiles and the playing of the organ. So I must go over tonight and see what all this is. And meantime I will scrawl a note to S. Young [Captain of School] enquiring what it is all about. (Have you still got my notes?)

Well I told the two men I thought little of the rugger outlook, that they must find a new scrum half, bring up Herbert from back into the middle, find a new back and teach the lot how to play...

While I was writing this, a telephone call says we beat Eastbourne 20-3 and 17-0, 1st and 2nd XVs respectively...

Now what other news is there? I've written to the Duchess of Kent to ask if she will revive the Feast Society. Her husband did in July 1939. It was founded in 1712 and functioned till about 1880. If she agrees it will be a potent assistance to the school's general development.

We have a new salary system which is very generous, and indeed rewards some more than they deserve. I have had the job this week of explaining to each man what he gets. It does not improve one's views of human nature. Under the old system, an odd man might have got an odd £50 p.a. for some odd job; now he gets his salary bumped up, say, by £200, & he wants both.

On Tuesday is the Governors' Meeting in London, & I think Maugham, Monty & all will be there. I have delivered an ultimatum in writing - either find another house for us in the Precincts or you must reduce by 25. This would mean £7000 less income & virtually that much less profit (since you can hardly save anything on the last 25). It would also mean that we sh'd have fewer vacancies, & applications easily in the ratio 2 to 1; thus I should have to take Scholars, and best payers, and there'd be no room for the Chapter's choristers on reduced fees. I expect there will be a colossal tussle.

Now I think, as it is nearing 6 o'c., the time, I understand, of this political meeting in the Parry, that I had better go over and see what it is all about. I have done so. There was a rowdy crowd, two others playing the organ (Brealy and Nye), Freyer on the platform in my chair, De Lisser prominent. It was a meeting to support the Conservatives. So, in the hush, I gently asked who was the Speaker. Freyer. So I mounted the platform and sat on the bench and said we would listen to Freyer make his speech. He hadn't got one; but began to read a pamphlet, at which I mildly protested but he explained that it was one of Churchill's and much better than any he could make. I agreed. So we sat in solemn silence while he read a lengthy speech of Churchill's, after which we gently applauded, & I made a few words that we'd now heard the Tory programme, & would go away wiser than we came (it might be), & De Lisser would see to the tidying of the Hall & lights and report to me when it was finished. So it was all a very damp squib, & I doubt we shall have any more political meetings. All the time Brealy and Nye had been waiting outside my study to be dealt with! I didn't, the results obtained being just as good...*

(Surely an object lesson in effective intervention without overkill.) I am still surprised that a very busy man found time to write at such length to a former pupil, and I am sure I was not uniquely favoured. At the same time one senses the enjoyment and amusement at the exercise of his talent for control. His passionate involvement in rugby football must have been a trial to coaches and captains. At home matches he patrolled the touchline on the school side, well away from visitors, staff and anyone whose proximity might have been inhibiting. Missed tackles or poor kicks and passes were greeted by hammering his stick on the ground, and he was apt to encroach on the field of play. One irritated captain of the XV had the temerity to order him off and, after the game, went to apologise, approaching the task with considerable apprehension. He found FJS chuckling with amusement and far from upset.

During the next few years of army service abroad and at university my contacts with him became perforce less frequent. I stayed a couple of times at Number 15 and recall a formidable written rebuke for not sending a proper letter of thanks to Mrs Shirley in due time. But he did not bear grudges.

Immediately after Cambridge I returned to Canterbury, only partially convinced of a vocation for teaching, still less that it was wise to come back. But I was immediately submerged in a full programme of teaching with a heavy sixth form commitment, coaching rowing and 'living in' as a house tutor. There was little time to prepare or plan lessons, still less to compensate for the lack of any formal teacher training or certification. I was also temporarily hard up. Salaries were paid termly in arrears and nobody had mentioned a figure. So it was a relief when one of the familiar cards appeared in my pigeon-hole with the usual initials and the single message:'£600 - O.K?'

* See also page 109

The school I rejoined seemed very different, and not just because of the shift in perspective. Numbers had risen by as much as a third; contrary to FJS's misgivings new houses had materialised; entries to Oxford and Cambridge continued to increase; the VIII had reached the Henley Final, fixture lists in cricket and rugby had widened and music was thriving as never before; there was soon a new setting for concerts and drama, including Headmaster's Assemblies, in the Great Hall, later named the Shirley Hall. The quality of a relatively young and energetic staff made for a stimulating atmosphere.

A year later, with even less preparation, I was catapulted into the housemastership of Galpin's. Seniority was never a factor to which FJS paid much if any attention. He probably enjoyed the ripples which appointments like this were bound to cause. I dare say my older colleagues were used to it, for they were extremely kind and tolerant, especially one or two who had real cause for disappointment.

As with housemasterships the selection and promotion of staff by FJS often seemed arbitrary and impulsive. Men of undoubted academic distinction, but temperamentally less suited to the ordinary run of teaching, were faced with recalcitrant Removes or weaker fifth form sets. Some like H R Dodd, a brilliant Germanist, found it impossible to convey much to the less gifted. H K ('Happy') Knight, a German scholar and theologian, was patently unhappy as a schoolmaster; his classes were notoriously unruly, yet FJS was most reluctant to part with him. (Some hinted that this was because his contribution to the headmaster's own scholarly treatises was vital.)

In academic terms it could be said that FJS was a traditionalist or, above all, a pragmatist. The school was geared to obtain the results which raised its standing against the all-important yardstick of the 'swell schools'. As in my own case boys specialised early, might spend four or five years in the sixth form and take Higher Certificate or A level several times, not to remedy failure but merely to repeat successes and to prepare for the university scholarship examinations. Breadth and balance were scarcely evident; the nearest I came to a science lesson was some astronomy in a general studies programme. Perhaps fortunately the extra-curricular life of the school was wide enough to offer some broader perspectives, notably in music and drama, though art, design and the manual crafts were not prominent in those days.

Within these limitations FJS did, however, give a free rein to talented staff. History and science under R W Harris and F Stanger respectively flourished as did classics and mathematics. Modern languages, with which I was primarily concerned both as pupil and teacher, struggled somewhat against the competition from a rampant history department. But it was a delight to study French literature with

F H Voigt and to work later alongside the linguistic flair of Keith Dickson, Richard Meredith and others. Men like these were increasingly encouraged to innovate and to drive up standards.

These were the last five years of his headmastership, outwardly crowned with greater success than ever, yet overshadowed by the inevitability of retirement and less satisfying, I am sure, than earlier times of striving and less fulfilled ambition. I was too busy myself to seek contact with him as I had done as a senior boy. Perhaps too, the more important lines of communication still ran as much to the Captain of School and, through him, to the monitors as to housemasters.

Bachelors were often preferred in houses to married men; they took less space and had fewer distractions. So my wish to marry, after three years in Galpin's, did pose a problem.

Monday. Private.

My dear Richard,

I have had the brain-wave of all time [in fact the idea started, I believe, with John Wilson, the Lower Master]. I would like you to take over Luxmoore for next Sept!! Now listen - that house is all-important - it is the most <u>seen</u> of all... I have made two foolish choices... can't afford a third... and it's all too serious to risk a lottery. It would be advantageous to you in affording more and better accommodation - gardens for the pram - nicer to live in in the holidays in all respects... I hope you will agree, for it would take a tremendous load of anxiety off my mind. F.J.S.

There was a familiar combination here of inducement and flattery. (Ironically, a year later, Neil Scott, a married man with children, moved into Galpin's which I had left with reluctance.)

Another persuasive letter contained further reference to his impending departure:

My dear Richard,

Don't, I beg you, make it hard for me, but I have got to ask you to squeeze in two more for next term! It is not my fault really - I didn't want to - but parents' pleas were so pitiful, & one or two O.K.S. at that, that I had really no option, unless I was to make the School seem very snotty... I know it's a bore, and not very easy; but things will soon be easier when I leave, which now draws very near!

There is a plan, as you know, for adding to the amenities of Luxmoore; and if the new fees 'take' and there's no evidence of cancellations, I expect the Governors will enlarge the place. Ideally, maybe they should enlarge both [buildings], and make two houses - I don't know; and anyhow that can wait on your own growing experience. Apart from that I should like to think of you as living at No.15; and why not? Pitt was Prime Minister at 24!

I've not been well this past fortnight... Love, F.J.S.

The idea of the succession and some other familiar themes occur in a letter written in response to my invitation for him to perform the baptism of our first child in the autumn of 1961:

My dear Richard,

Yes with great pleasure - Sept 16 - I ought to be back by then! You might drop a line to the Precentor and tell him that I'm doing the baptism...

I hope you and Keith [Dickson] will get a schol. or two this year... I'd like the biggest lot we've ever had! and since I've got Jim Parsons back [a huge youth who stayed on at school an extra year] I've got more hope of Henley.

You will, I hope, put in for the HMship, for I can, at least, guarantee you would be on the short list. I must move cannily and not show my hand, but I am moving alright. I ought to take you in hand about clothes and shoes, and see that you become nicely West End and hand-made! Strange that that sort of thing should count; but it does - anyway a little. Still you could afford it on £3000 a year and everything found. Mind, it won't be altogether an easy job, if you do take it on; for I believe it is the most difficult school in the country to administer, and ultimately you have to rely on the spirit and goodwill of the boys - for it is impossible to administer centrally by reason of the topographical situation and the fact that its physical extensions have been, perforce, haphazard, and the opposite of planned. But I think you could do it because you love it and would serve it...

And, of course, I should like you to be here because it would be happy for me. I shouldn't barge in - but you would still have me in your love a bit, whereas somebody else would regard me as an enemy, or at least a potential critic to be kept at a distance. Not that that can entirely be so, since the place is surrounded by governors whose ladies - if there are any - pick up most of the gossip that goes around; indeed, the holiday periods must be dull for them.

My love to you both, F.J.S.

In places the tone here reveals touches of pathos and insecurity in his reluctance to disengage; it also reflects his mischievous, even cynical humour. If it ever occurred to him that a retiring headmaster can perform a great service to his successor by moving well away, that was an option he was not prepared to contemplate. His hopes of influencing the succession were, of course, unrealistic. In the few years following his retirement it seemed that he did not, in fact, interfere as much as might have been expected. But he must have cast a long shadow.

From the perspective of my own retirement, after nearly 20 years as head of two smaller 'unswell' schools, his stature as a creative motivator remains immense. As an educationist or academic innovator he was less inventive, but often willing to give able men their head. Above all, it is the vitality and complexity of the man which lingers in the memory. He created an electric, often disturbing influence, even in his absence; but it was also an inspiration, a progressive driving force.

At the same time there was a dualism, even a plurality about him. On the one hand there was idealism: a strong, radical, iconoclastic, egalitarian side, an instinctive sympathy with the rebel, the awkward or brilliant boy, the aesthete or intellectual who might not fit a conventional mould. By contrast there was his willingness to manipulate boys and masters alike - and ruthlessly - if he believed it to be in the school's interests; and he exhibited an almost naive readiness (unless it was calculated or cynical) to be impressed by the social, intellectual, plutocratic or cultural pretensions of some in high places, though with his unwavering and often successful aim being to win their interest and support for the King's School.

Young men and boys who came under his spell had cause to be grateful for the challenges and opportunities he bestowed, often with rare trust, considering our inexperience. In later life we might wonder whether we had sometimes been offered more than was good for us at an impressionable age. The purple gowns, the court dress at Commemoration, the processions of surpliced King's Scholars, the shared confidences of an older man of power and experience, all made up a heady mixture for late adolescence. "We shall never feel so important again as long as we live," someone a year or two older than me said as he was leaving - and with some justification.

The exhilaration was stimulating and exciting but may also have brought later disillusion or disappointment. There were also many boys who, I expect, did not experience such opportunities or who felt left out. There were times when, in the role of headmaster myself, I struggled to suppress unrealistic comparisons between my own aims, achievements or style of leadership and those of FJS. Everyone who came into contact with him was measured, in his eyes, by their usefulness to the cause of the King's School, his cherished 'School', the word always with a capital 'S' when he wrote it. It was a judgment he would have extended equally to himself: I believe that he genuinely loved it and sought to serve it more than, as some allege, the repute it brought him. The school he left behind remains a living and evolving proof that he had indeed served it well, as much, at times, by his faults as by his virtues.

Edward Lucie-Smith

Edward Lucie-Smith, poet and art critic, was a pupil at the King's School, Canterbury, from 1946 to 1951. He went on from there to Merton College, Oxford, was an education officer in the Royal Air Force during his National Service and subsequently worked in advertising and as a free-lance journalist and broadcaster. His first book of poems, for which he won the John Llewellyn Rhys Memorial Prize, appeared in 1961. He is particularly noted as a writer of art books and his list of publications is extensive.

I arrived in Canterbury in 1946, aged 13. The war was over, the school had just returned from its wartime evacuation, we were on the eve of what was going to be one of the coldest winters in recent English history. It would be particularly cold in east Kent. And I came straight from the tropics. I had spent all of my life, with the exception of one brief interlude when I was five, when my parents were 'home on leave', in Jamaica where I had been born. I must have seemed, indeed in some respects I was, an odd, vulnerable little boy. I was bookish. I hated games, particularly any game involving a ball. Only much later did I discover that I had a quirk of eyesight, astigmatism, which explained this. Add to this the fact that I had a number of neurotic fads about food, and that I had been badly bullied about this and other quirks at my Jamaican prep school, and my transfer to a new country, and a new educational establishment, had all the makings of a disaster.

During my first few weeks at King's I kept my head down, trying to be as inconspicuous as possible. Nothing horrible happened to me, and gradually I began to look around. One day I drew a deep breath, and a triumphant inner voice said clearly: "Well, this lot are all soft." It spoke truly. Throughout the rest of my time at King's I benefited from a perhaps unlovable conviction that I would always get the better of any situation. My tough Jamaican prep school had taught me the arts of the ruthless machine politician, and (since adolescent boys have no consciences) I used them to the full.

It was at about this point - the time of my emergence from my shell - that Canon Shirley started to take an interest in me. I think there were several reasons. He was keen to build up the academic reputation of the school (later people would complain that he and his staff concentrated on the clever boys somewhat to the detriment of the rest) and it became clear that I had the makings of a high-flyer. I was extremely fluent, and also competitive. Examinations held no terrors for me: I took a certain pleasure in getting the better of any examiner. I was what schoolmasters think of as 'a delight to teach' - I sat in the front, asked the right questions, and absorbed information like blotting paper. On the rare occasions when my school fellows reproached me for this, I pointed out that if the teacher was concentrating on me, they had all the more liberty to do as they pleased in class. To each his own, in fact. As good headmasters should, Shirley tried to keep a finger on everything in the school, and news that I was a serious prospect for a major scholarship at Oxford or Cambridge soon got back to him.

To his credit, there was also something else. He was proud of the fact that the strange and the odd could flourish at King's without being molested. Much later I heard that he used to point me out as 'the kind of boy who can survive here', implying that I would have done so nowhere else. In this respect he seriously underestimated my streak of ruthlessness. I was feared rather than simply tolerated, not least because I had a knack for mobilising opinion and (in particular) for inventing nicknames. Few people crossed me twice.

For whatever reason, I interested him, and he took to summoning me to the headmaster's house for long chats: something he did with few other boys. At first I found these meetings alarming, later I began to find them entertaining, though I was always (rightly, I think) a little wary. Gradually they took on a particular character, that of the diplomatic exchange of information between two powers whose interests were not always identical. Shirley didn't want me to 'sneak' on other boys. He was far too subtle for that and too much aware of schoolboy conventions and notions of honour. He did want to find out what was going on in the school, and he knew that I knew many things that would interest him, which he would never get from his staff. Some I told him directly, others I told him through what was rather pointedly not said, and many more I prudently suppressed. Trying to extract information, he would poke me in the midriff with a bony finger, addressing me, as he addressed all boys, as "m'dear". This verbal mannerism was often mimicked.

The room in which these colloquies took place was large and sunny, on the ground floor of the official Canon's residence the Shirleys occupied. On the walls was a fine collection of Rowlandson drawings: they would cause a sensation at auction today, and there were other good things scattered about. I was already interested in art and in antiques. These objects were an education in themselves .

Shirley did in fact have excellent, if middle-brow, taste in all the arts. The musical evenings he occasionally arranged at the school were of an unusually good standard. The first piece of classical music I consciously enjoyed was the aria 'Where'er you walk' from Handel's *Semele*, sung on this occasion by Dennis Noble. It was not until much

104

later that I caught the opera-bug, but this was a first step. Shirley courted famous personalities, and got them to come and talk to the boys. Some had been 'old boys', though their connection with King's was sometimes rather tenuous: Field Marshal Montgomery, for example, had attended the one-time junior school and only for a short period. He arrived outrageously late, in a flashy 1930s Rolls-Royce. Somerset Maugham was persuaded to renew his links with an institution where he had been very unhappy. I remember him sitting - can it have been on a tall stool, or is my memory corrupted by the image of him in the celebrated Graham Sutherland portrait? - in the midst of a circle of boys, looking like an uneasy and discontented tortoise. Vita Sackville-West came from Sissinghurst to give a poetry reading. She was very tall and gaunt and wore a large hat and a formidable moustache. When she declaimed, the boys could scarcely suppress their giggles. John Betjeman also came to read his poetry, and I was persuaded (it did not take much persuasion) to give him my own early efforts. He wrote me a marvellous letter, kind, sensible and encouraging, which I unfortunately lost.

With Shirley a Canon and not simply the headmaster of the school, the links during his time with the Cathedral were especially close. He was not the only powerful personality in the Chapter. Its most celebrated member was the notorious Red Dean, Dr Hewlett Johnson, an enthusiastic fellow-traveller and an embarrassment to the Archbishop, Dr Fisher, as well as to his colleagues. Schoolboys are great gossips, and also great voyeurs. They love anything that has the makings of a drama. We avidly watched the comings and goings of the Chapter, and those of the Dean in particular. It was generally understood that Shirley and Johnson were rivals, each continually striving for supremacy in Cathedral affairs. Shirley felt that the Dean's left-wing inclinations might prejudice people against the school, and he endeavoured to reduce contact to a minimum. Boys who insisted on consorting with the Dean - I can think of one in particular, the school communist, now a respectable solicitor - never met with his approval.* On the other hand, he had to be diplomatic about his opposition. He was not best pleased when I made a rather telling linocut caricature of Dr Johnson (a back view, bandy-legged and wearing gaiters) and published it in the lavishly produced school magazine, *The Cantuarian*, which I edited.

In retrospect, Shirley and Johnson were in many respects alike: flamboyant, rather worldly ecclesiastics, who might have stepped from the pages of a novel by Trollope. Shirley's redfaced, slightly agricultural appearance (one could at a distance have mistaken him for a prosperous farmer) makes the comparison especially apt. Neither man, interestingly enough, was a really good preacher, though the

* See also page 78

105

Dean was, in general, better than Shirley. Even now it is difficult to put one's finger on the reason why the latter's sermons were ineffective. They were not intellectual - but in any case that would have been unsuited to their intended audience. But they were also curiously unmoving. Shirley's most conspicuous vocal mannerisms - his characteristic nasal swoops, which nowadays would perhaps be described as 'camp' - were suppressed for the occasion, but there was little sense of fervour, or spiritual conviction. In the magnificent setting of the great Romanesque and Gothic church, his homilies sounded irrelevant and out of place.

What did the boys think of Fred? They undoubtedly respected him for his commitment to the school. They appreciated his shrewdness, good sense and sense of fair play. They also liked his actor-ish, hammy side. What they mocked most was what seemed to them his snobbery and his social-climbing. But you could never be quite sure that this wasn't itself put on, exaggerated for the sake of effect. He was notorious for his shameless appeals for money. One term, I and a couple of collaborators put on an ambitious pantomime, with original words and music. The hit number was sung by a Canon Shirley figure:

> I'm a poor bewildered canon,
> Torn in half 'twixt God and Mammon,
> Ah, will no-one pity me!

The headmaster's devoted secretary, Miss Milward, who resembled an elderly Highland terrier, was outraged at our disrespect. Shirley himself sat in the centre of the front row and laughed uproariously. He was, I think, perfectly genuinely amused.

The quality about him which I failed to recognise at the time - I was more sophisticated than most of my schoolfellows, but still not sophisticated enough for that - was a fundamental and rather admirable detachment. He was committed to the school, but not necessarily to the aggrandisement of his own ego. Looking back, I think he saw himself as I see him now, as a very skilful actor, gleefully carrying off the major role in some play. Between his true self and the successful headmaster there was a small but important area of separation.

Queen Salote of Tonga visits King's in 1953, Coronation year.

Ralph Blumenau

Ralph Blumenau emigrated from Nazi Germany in 1936. He was educated at St Paul's School and Wadham College, Oxford. He taught history at the King's School, Canterbury, in 1951 and from 1953 to 1957. From 1957 until retirement in 1985 he was head of history and general studies at Malvern College. Since then he has been teaching at the University of the Third Age in London.

The education section of Oxford University's appointments board was presided over by a dreadful snob called A R Woolley. Fairly early on in my interview with him he had ascertained that I was Jewish, and the following dialogue ensued:

Woolley: "Are you a believing Jew?"

R.B: "No, I'm not. I have no religion."

Woolley: "H'm. You'll have a problem getting a job at a decent public school."

I do not know what he subsequently wrote to Canon Shirley but I was invited to go and see him in December 1950 for a job the following September. In the course of my interview he said, "I expect all my staff to attend our Sunday service in the Cathedral. Would you have objections to that?" I said that, if he was willing to accept that I would only be going through the motions, I would have no objections. I was offered the post and his parting shot was, "Try to get a teaching job for the next two terms, so that you can rub off some of the rough edges before you come to us."

Thus it was that after a temporary position at King's School, Gloucester, I arrived to take up my post in Canterbury. The contrasts were marked, and King's, Canterbury, was a world apart from Gloucester: the boys were bright and a joy to teach; the school was among the top half dozen for Oxford and Cambridge awards; it boasted two orchestras, drama of top quality and the King's Week festival at the end of each summer term.

It quickly became clear that the ruthless driving force behind all this was Shirley. He was responsible for all that was best in the school; but I also found him its most detestable feature. He was a capricious and manipulative tyrant, a true Machiavellian who could charm when he wanted to but who had perfected techniques of intimidation, indulged in shameless but temporary favouritism, encouraged sycophancy, fostered a system of tale-bearing, loved playing people off against each other and stopped at no guile to get his way.

Shirley knew everything that went on at the school and no one was allowed any independence. He contemptuously set aside all conventions of seniority; young bachelors who had shown themselves biddable were appointed as housemasters after only a few years at the school, and it was made clear to them that biddable bachelors they were expected to remain. If a housemaster married he was expected to leave the house (none of the houses had a 'private side', quarters which would have used up accommodation for boys). An exception to this was made for one favoured housemaster, but when he married he was ordered to have no children! Shirley's aim was to squeeze everything he possibly could out of his staff, and young men without family obligations could be expected to give their all to the school.

Shirley undoubtedly had the ambition to make King's the finest school in the country, and it is true that he gave everything to that end which was, of course, simultaneously to serve his own self-aggrandisement and vanity. The senior history master, R W Harris, aptly compared him to Louis XIV at Versailles. Shirley had the same desire for *la gloire*; the staff were his cowed and sycophantic nobles, spied and reported on by the senior boys; and he would have identified with Louis' dictum that *l'état, c'est moi*. Each year the head monitor would organise a collection of money for a sizeable headmaster's birthday present; and the school learned to perform for his pleasure: the first words of actors after the final fall of the curtain or of rugger players at the end of a match were, "What do you think Fred thought of it?" They were pleased when he was pleased, and they dreaded his anger when their performance fell below his expectations.

In my first Canterbury term I was very much in Shirley's good books and was too enthralled with the school to let the headmaster's personality impinge too much upon me. Even so, however, I had two experiences of him which were both in their own way characteristic. The first was during the 1951 general election: the boys had organised their own mock election to which I went along as the only master present. Now, a similar event had been staged for the 1950 election and the communist candidate had done very well - he may even have won. The local paper had reported this and had linked it up with the fact that the chairman of the school's governors was Hewlett Johnson, the Red Dean. Shirley had been furious; he disliked the Dean, had carried on a rather childish vendetta against him and was worried about the misconceptions that could be aroused by Hewlett Johnson's connections with the school.

When Shirley heard about this second mock election he stormed into the meeting just as the senior boy (his name was Freyer) standing as the Conservative candidate was being boisterously and noisily heckled. "How dare you," he roared, and there was immediately a stunned silence. He raged on, seemingly quite out of control. Just then a small new boy came in late carrying an enormous cardboard box. "You, there!" Shirley shouted, "What have you got in that box?" "Oranges, sir," squeaked the poor youth. "My mother sent them to me." "Is she in the Conservative interest too?" Shirley sneered inconsequentially. At this point he noticed that I was in the hall and perhaps realised what an exhibition he was making of himself. "Well," he said sardonically, "You've come to hear the Conservative candidate; so let's hear what he has to say," and he sat down, folded his arms and glared at the youth.

The candidate now no longer had the nerve to *ad lib* as he had intended. Fortunately he had with him the local candidate's election manifesto which, he said falteringly, expressed Conservative ideas better than he could himself, and he went on to read this out, which he did in stony silence from the audience. There was more silence at the end which Shirley allowed to last for several seconds. He then gave a perfunctory clap or two and said, "Well, Freyer is right; he couldn't have done better than that himself. So now you've heard what you've come to hear, you can all go." And the hall emptied in complete silence. The next day Shirley told me that I would be wise to keep more distance from the boys.*

The other incident refers to a class I was teaching. I was allowed to take the Oxbridge scholarship set for some general periods and was apparently given freedom by Shirley to do with them whatever I wanted. On one occasion I read them an extract from *The Screwtape Letters* which explored the thesis that science had emancipated itself from nineteenth century materialism and that in the twentieth century many scientists had been led by their subject to a belief in God. The class and I then had a discussion as to why science had become less materialist in the twentieth century. By the next morning Shirley had heard from one of the boys about this lesson, and I found one of his famous little cards in my pigeon hole: 'History, yes; Literature, yes; Philosophy, yes; anything to broaden the youthful mind. But Theology, I think not! FJS'.

After a term at King's I succumbed to the temptation of what turned out to be an *ignis fatuus* and successfully applied for the directorship of a youth institute being set up in Germany by UNESCO, and Shirley released me. (I learned later that UNESCO had mobilised the Ministry of Education to put pressure on Shirley to allow me to go. He had, characteristically, struck a bargain with them: for a long time he had been waiting for authority to build a new range of classrooms; the permits were swiftly granted.) Sadly the post turned out to be no bed of roses, and after eight months I resigned and returned to England. Again I visited the egregious A R Woolley.

Woolley: "H'm. You know as a Jew you will find it difficult to get a job at a decent public school."

R.B: "I remember your telling me this last time; but perhaps I could remind you that I was appointed by Canon Shirley, DD, of the King's School, Canterbury."

Woolley: "Ah yes; but then we all know that Canon Shirley is a man of no principles."

His views of Shirley were probably confirmed when in due course, after a year teaching in a prep school, I was re-appointed to the King's staff.

I returned anxious that one day I would fulfil an ambition and be made a housemaster. Looking back I realise what a bed of nails it would have been. Shirley regarded and treated his housemasters as little better than senior prefects - and indeed used prefects and senior boys as his informants, encouraging them to come to him with complaints about their housemasters and in this way systematically undermining the housemaster's authority. When complaints came his way he would interfere, and housemasters could not rely on the backing of a headmaster to whom the concept of loyalty was completely alien and who seemed to take positive pleasure in keeping them in cowed dependence on him. Housemasters held their positions entirely at his whim and enjoyed no sort of security of tenure. In 1954, within the space of two terms, two housemasters were forced to resign because Shirley considered that they did not get on well enough with their senior boys.

My relationship with Shirley was the one that dominated my Canterbury life. Soon after I returned he called me in one evening for the sole purpose of telling me how exercised he was about the world's needless suffering and cruelty and how his faith was profoundly shaken by it all. It was as if he was using me, whom he knew to be a humanist, as a kind of confessor. One particular event had particularly devastated him. A pupil in the school was slowly dying of cancer. During Lent it was Shirley's wont to have friars and the like visiting the school. Three weeks after my 'confessional' meeting with him he invited an American revivalist preacher, Pastor Roland Brown. The whole school had an afternoon free of lessons to hear this man preach an unbelievably crude and 'hammy' sermon. Shirley had told him about the boy with cancer, and Pastor Brown said that he would save him by prayer. Senior boys were summoned to the headmaster's house, and there they and Shirley knelt as Pastor Brown prayed with them for the poor boy's life. Nine days later Shirley shakily told the school at assembly that the boy had died. It is always a traumatic experience for a school when one of its pupils dies; but it was particularly so in this case when such an air of religious hysteria had been whipped up in the school for days beforehand.*

Shirley's own sermons were often powerful and emotional. He himself lavishly committed most of the Seven Deadly Sins (except perhaps Gluttony), and I was also fairly certain that, when he preached eloquently against one of them, it was because he had just been guilty of it - just as I am convinced that each night he went down on his knees tremblingly begging his Maker for forgiveness.

He was not, however, forgiving to boys who 'cut' Cathedral. The headmaster's noticeboard carried his typical cryptic notes: a mere list of names without any other indication meant that the boys on it were to come and see him. Sometimes he would look through the school list and realise that he could not put a face to one of the new boys' names, and that was the reason for the listed summons; but the little lad would be in fear and trembling lest he had done something to incur the headmaster's wrath. Older boys feared another list featuring name, number and offence, the number indicating how many strokes of the cane had been administered. Within one term there appeared three such notices: six boys were given ten each for cutting a class; three were given ten for cutting Cathedral; two more were given 12 for the same offence. (This sadism is one of the reasons why I acquit Shirley only of Gluttony and not of Lust.)

A frequent implication of his sermons was that godlessness, lack of moral fibre and personal worthlessness were closely connected. This I found not only absurd but also damaging to sensitive boys who could not believe. I wrote a long letter to Shirley (today its somewhat ingratiating tone makes me cringe) advancing my point. He wrote back to say that it was unanswerable, admitted how he had let such boys down and promised to atone. Encouraged by this, the following term I even sent him notes for a sermon which I suggested that he might care to use.

Why did I do all this? Like most of the staff and all the boys I was caught up in the urge to be in Shirley's good books. We were all contemptible courtiers of an unpredictable despot. But in particular I hoped to be able to persuade Shirley that, despite my not being a Christian, I could safely be entrusted with a housemastership.

It was Shirley's philosophy to work his staff to the limit. He saw the school magazine, *The Cantuarian*, for which he gave me responsibility, not only as a powerful advertisement for the school but also as a vehicle to promote his own views and interests. On a few occasions he asked me to write articles on themes which he wanted to promulgate. For example, he rightly detested the Canterbury development plan to replace the bombed medieval buildings with characterless modern

* See also page 60

structures; I was ordered to write a piece attacking the authorities. He had instigated the opening up of a crypt chapel and the revealing of its twelfth century frescoes; I was to write this up in a scholarly way.

The worst 'hack' work which I did for him was to lend myself to Shirley's continuing campaign against Hewlett Johnson. Shirley was anxious lest parents or others outside the school assumed that the Red Dean's views on the wonders of the Soviet Union were somehow the opinions of the school. I was ordered to write a *Cantuarian* editorial condemning the 1956 Russian invasion of Hungary and the Dean's defence of it. I felt strongly about this myself, but all the same it was a 'hatchet' job, with Shirley touching up some of my phrases to give them a more vicious point. Even as I was writing it I felt shame, the more so when the national press reprinted part of it. Above all I was ashamed that I had lacked the courage to refuse Shirley's instruction and to tell him that, if he wanted to attack his chairman of governors, he do it in his own name and not shelter behind unsigned editorials (which were customarily written by boys).

One of Shirley's techniques in making mischief was to give the same job to two masters and to suggest to each that he was in charge. Towards the end of one term, when I asked one of the *Cantuarian* boy-editors why I had not yet had any material to look at, he replied that the headmaster had told him to submit it to another member of staff. This particular limp and pathetic clergyman, with weakness and failure written all over him, had done some writing for Shirley who, out of pity (he was capable of doing quixotic and impulsive things like that), had appointed him to the school. He was incapable of controlling a class, and Shirley must have looked round for another task to give the man and told him to take charge of *The Cantuarian*.

Copying the style of Shirley's cryptic little notes, I wrote to him, 'I take note of the fact, brought to my knowledge by a boy, that you have relieved me of my responsibilities with regard to *The Cantuarian*'. He replied, 'I have not the slightest knowledge of what you are talking about and perhaps you will be good enough to explain to me tomorrow'. When I nervously turned up he seized me by the front of my shirt, snarled that he resented the tone of my note, denied everything and demanded to know who my boy informant was. "I'll have his guts," he roared. His long-suffering secretary, the dour Miss Milward, was present during this scene. Later that day she told me that she had reminded the headmaster that he had in her presence told the other member of staff to take charge of *The Cantuarian*. In the evening I had a note from Shirley, almost apologetic and containing a long self-pitying moan about how overworked he was, how charitable, how ill... It was a typical episode.

In 1957 I was approached about a senior history post elsewhere, just when I was much exercised about the possibility of becoming a housemaster at King's. I felt that I must clarify my prospects and wrote to Shirley about them. He kept me on tenterhooks for three days before replying and telling me that I could do a lot of valuable pastoral work at King's, but on religious grounds I could not expect a house. I was more shaken than I should have been by his response and suddenly felt the strongest wish to leave the school. Not the least reason was the knowledge that, once Shirley knew that a member of staff was seeking another post, he tended to ascribe this to dissatisfaction and would make life difficult if the new job did not transpire. I was fortunate: Malvern wanted a man who would take over the history department in two years, and I was appointed just in time to give Shirley the required term's notice.

I was at the time deeply saddened to leave a school where the academic and artistic standards were so high and the setting so beautiful and historic. Shirley could legitimately take the credit for the great achievements at King's, but my view was (and still is) that the price he made the entire community pay was profoundly degrading. Mark 8.36 says it all: For what shall it profit a man, if he shall gain the whole world, and lose his own soul?

A visit from Somerset Maugham in 1958. Although he had had an unhappy time as a pupil at King's, Maugham subsequently became a benefactor and an honoured guest during Canon Shirley's headmastership.

1960, and 25 years at King's. Mrs Shirley plants a commemorative tree.

JR Painter looks on (rather obsequiously)

John Wilson

John Wilson was educated at Winchester and New College, Oxford. In 1953 he was appointed to the staff of the King's School, Canterbury, and subsequently became a housemaster and then Lower Master. After leaving King's in 1961 he became successively Professor of Religion at Trinity College, Toronto, Lecturer in Philosophy at the University of Sussex and Director of the Farmington Trust at Oxford. He is now Senior Research Associate at the Oxford University Department of Educational Studies. He is the author of many books in the field of education, philosophy and personal relationships.

I worked for, and in some sense with, Shirley between 1953 and 1961. After my first year at King's I took over a boarding house whose general rebelliousness had made the previous housemaster's position untenable; and some years after that I was elevated to the giddy rank of Lower Master, above the heads of older and worthier candidates. I resigned when he retired. So I may be *parti pris*: certainly by these appointments he afforded me the chance of some interesting, if not to say hectic, experiences. But the experience of Shirley himself was by far the most valuable.

I think I knew when being interviewed (if you can call it that) at Oxford for what was to be my first job that I was in for an unorthodox relationship. After a good many glasses of whisky he asked me - it was his only question - what I thought of buggery. I temperately replied that I was, on the whole, against it. "H'm," he replied, "buggers really make the best schoolmasters though." I muttered something about Plato's *Symposium* and we had yet another glass. And though his sexual life was, at least in its strictly physical aspects, entirely above reproach, that set the tone for most of our subsequent conversations: no holds were barred, no conventions taken for granted, anything went. I found this refreshing, if sometimes difficult.

That sort of unconventionality might have been boring and unproductive had Shirley not possessed more charisma than anyone I have met before or since. 'Charisma' is a name for nothing clear; but I saw him exercise a magnetic influence time and again over people of both sexes and all ages and backgrounds. I see myself as naturally contra-suggestible, but I had to fight, sometimes quite hard, to remember that this was a man and not some kind of demonic force. It was nothing like hero-worship, though for the simple-minded it might take that form. It was more like being with someone who, at whatever particular time one came across him, was entirely possessed with some particular aim or mood or passion, who reserved nothing of himself in the way that most of us do. And though, as history shows, this characteristic worked out to the great benefit of the school, it had in itself nothing that one would describe as 'good' or 'bad' in strictly moral terms.

One anecdote amongst many may clarify this. My house put on a perhaps faintly risqué play (I think by Noel Coward) in the Chapter House and attended by Shirley and other Cathedral Canons. During the first act Shirley was laughing his head off, entirely engrossed. But in the interval one dignitary had a word in his ear to the effect that the play perhaps bordered on the indecent or inappropriate. Immediately and totally Shirley's attitude changed: there were scowls and snorts of disapproval and at one point he made as if to walk out. In a subsequent interview with me both these conflicting attitudes surfaced: for some minutes he relived the play with delight, revelling retrospectively in the risqué jokes, but then his expression completely changed, a different daemon took over and he became the stern moralist and guardian of the mores of the young.

He had, I am quite sure, no awareness of this at all. It was like a psychiatrist who, having evoked a powerful transference with his client, takes absolutely no notice of it but just uses it to gain his ends. Nor were the ends with Shirley always deviously utilitarian. On several occasions I came upon him racked with what appeared to be guilt and fear, having had bad dreams. "Is there really an after-life, John; what do you think? Shall we be saved?" I found myself putting an arm round him and comforting him: "Yes, yes, we shall be saved; it'll be all right." And when he rejoiced at having put one over on some obstructer or enemy, it was almost impossible not to imitate his slightly malicious smile.

One naturally felt ambivalent to such a person. Some people - and I do not sneeze at them - either hated and feared him deeply (and usually left the school pretty quickly) or else swallowed him whole and more or less worshipped him. One could survive, as I did, if one controlled the ambivalence and remembered that the job was what really counted in the long run. One also had to remember that one could work for him and sometimes (for he was often absent or just plain bored) instead of him, but not in any serious sense with him. (This was made plain to me early on when all the members of some committee decided firmly that X was the thing to be done, after which Shirley, who had been sitting entirely silent throughout, told us that what was actually going to happen was Y. So much for democracy, consultation, participation!)

One had also to accept unorthodoxy. A good example here comes from David Edwards's essentially pietistic biography [*F.J. Shirley: An*

Extraordinary Headmaster, published in 1969], a useful work which fails - it does not try - to capture what Shirley was really like. In the book is reprinted a sermon preached by Shirley in Canterbury Cathedral. It does not mention that it was written by myself at his request (perhaps I should say, command). My view on that is, and was, that it requires much more talent to get someone else to write one's sermons than to write them oneself. Shirley had in fact an exaggerated idea of my intellect when compared with his own, and I was more than happy to cash in on this. No doubt I was flattered; but it was more than that: it seemed somehow impossible to refuse such a person.

I do not know enough about Shirley's childhood or background to make any guesses as to where this charisma came from, but there is no doubting its strength. After he retired he sent me a vast quantity of his private correspondence; hero worship, or some kind of transference, was everywhere to be seen. I was immediately put in mind of Thomas Arnold, the 'great doctor' with whom many of his pupils were, in effect, in love. Arnold - despite his old-fashioned Victorian image - and Shirley had much in common.

Shirley raises an important educational question: what sort of figure a headmaster should cut, what kind of transference (if any) he should seek to generate and how he should handle it. Shirley did not really handle it at all; he just acted it out. Most of the time, but not always, it worked well. Up to the mid 1950s he could hold the whole school spellbound in assembly. (This was not always done by magniloquence or magnetism; sometimes just by jokes. "Though I speak with the tongues of men and of angels," read out a stuttering school monitor incompetently. "Neither," said Shirley in an audible mutter to be heard by all.) After that time the school clientèle became, at least in part, too sophisticated to be sufficiently suggestible and some of his later 'acts' failed to cut ice.

My own view is that this kind of charisma is quite essential for any serious education. At least something actually happened in the emotional lives of pupils and staff (and indeed almost anyone with whom he came into contact). There was a chance for emotional growth. Admittedly there were favourites or devotees who were more or less taken over, but no more so than by a powerful parent: those whose psychology needed a god or father-figure found one in him (and in his received correspondence it is hard to distinguish the two). Others were at least shaken out of their smug skins. Of course the fashion has changed: headmasters are now - no doubt they have to be - more bland, more orthodox, more concerned with public relations, all things to all men and with their personalities and emotions thickly screened behind the role. They may even have read books on 'management' and 'pastoral care'!

Shirley was the antithesis of political correctness. When he put up a notice about a boy whom he was about to beat - 'Smith, 12, for causing me trouble' - or when after a term he sent me a note saying simply '£100 more pay next term for being a good boy' he was acting as a parent. These actions are today unthinkable and to avoid abuses we have outlawed corporal punishment and have fixed salary scales. The climate has changed but it is clear that something too has been lost.

Unlike most of us today Shirley was not frightened of either his sexuality or his aggression. He demonstrably liked fair hair and blue eyes (which I suspect accounted for my quaintly meteoric rise even more than my having a First in Greats) and was more than willing to engage in conversations which, if not precisely locker-room, were at least unusual for that time. ("What's this I hear about you and - - -?" "Well, sir, er, I..." "Yes, I see she's attractive, old man; of course I see that, but just a bit suburban, wouldn't you say?") He was also quite happy to fly into rages, almost tantrums, when possessed by that particular daemon, and showed no particular guilt or other after-effects. ("You bloody man, why the hell have you...?" One just had to sit these out and hope that normal communication would be resumed as soon as possible.)

This incidentally - perhaps his most obvious 'moral' merit in the narrow sense of 'moral' - made him entirely sympathetic ('compassionate' is too weak a word) with those whose own sexuality or aggression had landed them in trouble. He related to homosexuals, for instance, rather than just being tolerant or pitying (or disapproving). He was, I think, by nature multisexual (what Freud called 'polymorphous') and it is fortunate for us as well as for him that he was able to control his overt sexual behaviour. And he also controlled - but only just - his aggression, keeping it more or less within orthodox bounds. Like many really good teachers who are also parent-figures he would not, I think, have found it easy to survive today. The orthodoxy is too strong and we are too frightened.

Or perhaps one should rather say that he was very closely in touch with his physical or sensual self. A heavy smoker, sometimes a heavy drinker, he also delighted in music (preferably not of the fa-la-la type) and acting or directing on stage. He had an excellent ear and memory for rhythms and could recite whole swathes of poems like *The Ingoldsby Legends*. That kind of sensuality, if that is the right word, was an essential part of his charisma: he did not retreat from his basic desires and feelings but just used them to the full. And that too is something of which most of us are frightened.

Such characters as Shirley are apt to produce a split in those who know or remember them. With one part of ourselves we stand in admiration, almost awe, at the achievements (it is easy to be pietistic about 'a great headmaster'). With another part we smile in a slightly guilty or underhand way at some of the unorthodoxies (and around Shirley innumerable more or less amusing anecdotes abound): 'the great man' had his jokes, his weaknesses, his feet of clay. There is an analogy here with Churchill and Lloyd George: heroes but with their 'human' side.

But I do not believe that Shirley's greatness lies in this mixture of public achievement and private entertainment value (though both are undeniable). It lies - to put the point in a rather prissy psychological way - in the fact that he had more of himself available in consciousness than do the rest of us, and he could make use of what he had available. To talk of his being able to 'sublimate' his sexuality and aggression hardly does it justice; we all have to do that somehow. Certainly he 'sublimated' them in the sense of putting them to good use, not only for the benefit of the school - that might have got successfully off the ground in other hands, as it now flies successfully in other hands - but perhaps more importantly for the benefit of innumerable individuals (he knew all members of the school by name). But the real point is that he just had more of himself available to 'sublimate' or to use. He operated consistently near 100% while the rest of us operate only at about 50%, rising to 60% on one of our good mornings. And that is a rarer, and more important, gift than most others in an educator.

Tristan Garel-Jones

The Rt Hon Tristan Garel-Jones was a pupil at the Junior King's School, Canterbury, prior to joining the Senior School in 1954. He left in 1960 and was principal of the family language school in Madrid before becoming a merchant banker. He was elected Member of Parliament for Watford in 1979 and subsequently held various Government offices including that of Minister of State, Foreign and Commonwealth Office.

Like all boys at King's in Dr Shirley's time I very much felt that I was part of a school on the move and going places. His dynamism and drive impinged strongly on us all.

Two particular memories stand out. One is the Queen Mother's visit to open the new hall (school assemblies henceforth moved from the Chapter House), and I can remember that occasion clearly (it was the first time I wore a morning coat!) as Shirley escorted her round the Precincts. The other is of him and rugger: on the touchline, walking up and down, waving his stick around and getting frightfully excited about the matches.

Indeed, the rugby was the cause of one of my few personal encounters with him. He had seen me playing in the house leagues (these were the lowest of the low), and one day, as I was cycling to play squash on Blore's, he was watching the 1st and 2nd XVs on a pre-season practice. For some reason he was displeased. I was hauled off my bike and literally thrown into the top squad. In fact the first time I ever represented the school in any sort of rugger match was in the 1st XV, which was unusual if not unique.

His knowledge of what was going on was huge. Although I am unable to vouch for the details I do recall, I think, that one evening I was asked for matches or cigarettes as the Headmaster had run out! An oblique way of his letting me know that *he* knew that I was a smoker.

I believe that every boy was aware that Shirley had picked up the school, that he had almost physically dragged it from its knees into the first division and that we were all part of an enterprise which was forging ahead.

And a final image? It has to be Shirley at a school rugger match, never quite able to stand on the touchline like everyone else, always a few yards in on the field of play; the white tie at his collar and the stick waving; calling, almost pulling the boys along, bringing such a sense of commitment to the whole thing. This for me is the abiding memory.

John Batchelor

Professor John Batchelor went as a King's Scholar to the King's School, Canterbury, in 1955. He gained an entrance scholarship to Magdalene College, Cambridge, where he read first history and then English. After a year on a research fellowship in Canada at the University of New Brunswick he returned to Cambridge, completing his doctorate in 1969. He was a lecturer in English at the University of Birmingham from 1968 to 1976, in which year he was elected as a Tutorial Fellow of New College, Oxford. In 1990 he was appointed to the Joseph Cowen Chair of English Literature at the University of Newcastle. His many publications include books on Virginia Woolf and H G Wells. He is general editor of the World's Classics edition of the works of Joseph Conrad (Oxford University Press) and his The Life of Joseph Conrad: A Critical Biography *was published by Blackwell in 1994 (paperback 1996). He is now writing an intellectual biography of John Ruskin.*

Monsters are often great leaders, great leaders are often monsters. Fred was both. Muriel Spark's *The Prime of Miss Jean Brodie*, that chillingly intelligent black farce about the way forceful teachers can impact upon impressionable children, expresses (with an appropriate change of gender) many of my feelings about Fred. My perception of him is double - the alarming and inappropriate intimacy with which this pebble-lensed, plumpish, red-faced person liked to gossip to favoured teenage boys about his supposed enemies among the school staff (Fred clearly had no time for such wimpish virtues as solidarity and professional loyalty) and the conscious grandeur with which he took over the Cathedral services and used his considerable powers of oratory to impress the grander parents and the better-connected boys. His contempt for loyalty was matched by his blatant enjoyment of the trappings of office: he was like a Borgia pope, and the Cathedral was widely known, for good reasons, as 'Shirley's Temple'.

I was brought into uncomfortably close contact with Fred when he chose to direct the school Shakespeare play one summer in the Archdeacon's garden. He chose *Twelfth Night*. I was required to play Olivia - a thoroughly thankless role for a teenage boy (Shakespeare's boy actors must have loathed it). Fred was undeterred by his grotesquely complete absence of qualification or aptitude for the role of theatre director. One of his decisions about my performance was that I needed to 'project'. (I was a bit inhibited by the fact that my Olivia obviously had a bass voice and took size nine in high-heeled slippers.) I persisted in my failure to 'project', and Fred resorted to physical coercion which was both comically exaggerated and frighteningly real (I dare say Saddam Hussein uses similar methods). He would stand behind one on the stage with an open pen-knife in his hand and say, "There is a deaf old lady in the back row. She has *paid* to come to King's Week to hear you. Speak as loud as you can and, if I can't hear your consonants, I am going to insert this pen-knife until I *can* hear your consonants."

He also felt (rightly) that my performance lacked romantic passion. "You are supposed to be *in love* with Cesario, to have passionate feelings for him. Have you never had passionate feelings for other young men in the school?" And, with a worldly air of stating the obvious: "It's not unknown in all-male communities, m'dear." (All Fred imitations among the boys included the phrase 'm'dear'. John Wilson, Lower Master, told me that it was a phrase that he had never heard Fred actually use, but he certainly used it to me.) The wretched rehearsals dragged on, my Olivia got no better, and Fred threatened to sack me: "You look all right, but you're entirely without any emotion. I could play the part myself better than you do." I took this to be a joke and then I saw that he actually meant it - he fancied himself dressed up as Olivia *à la* Queen Elizabeth I (in a red wig and a high lace collar festooned with fake pearls), and he genuinely thought that he could carry it off. It was on that hot summer afternoon in the Precincts in June 1957 that I decided that Fred was not just outrageous and alarming but, at a deep level, mad.

The power games were part of the madness. If he had had a row with a member of his staff he had no hesitation in discussing this with one of his inner circle of favourite boys. I was part of that inner circle for a year or so (although I didn't recognise at the time that this was what the situation was). Much of his venom was aimed at his housemasters, whom he saw as cautious, suburban, dim and obstinate. Fred would come out with lines like "There are five headmasters in this school, did you know that?" or "The trouble with this school is not the parents, it's not the boys, it's not sex, it's the *over-forties*."

Confidences from distressed colleagues were invitations, in Fred's eyes, to engage in mischievous indiscretion with his favourites. The Cathedral archivist, the late William Urry, had obviously taken Fred into his confidence about his despair over what he felt to be his stalled career. I used to go in a small group of the history upper sixth to William Urry for lessons in palaeography, and one afternoon I found myself in Fred's house with Fred consulting me (aged 17!) about Urry's career frustration. "Urry's *wet*," declared Fred. "He has no ambition. He says to me that R W Harris [the remarkable and brilliant historian who was the school's Master of Studies] is doing better than he is. And I say to him, 'But you're not Harris; you don't have Harris's energy and drive.' And I'll show you what I've done, I've hung the doctoral cap and gown up on a hook in Urry's room and I said to him, 'There! That's your target! Work for that!' " The interesting thing about this bullying behaviour is that - as was often the case with Fred's steam-roller approach to other people's problems - it *worked*. Urry's distinguished research enabled him to escape from the Cathedral library to a career in Oxford as Reader in Palaeography.

Simple games of colleague-baiting were irresistible to Fred. One way in which he could tease and unsettle the average schoolmaster on his staff was by encouraging exotic favourites whose visits to the school produced minor but vexatious disorder, like a series of small but obdurate bush fires, among the boys. One of these *protégés* was Malcolm Burgess, an Old Boy of King's who was at that time an assistant lecturer in Russian at Cambridge, and who kept close links with the school. Among Malcolm's many gifts was an outstanding flair for stage design, and it was Malcolm who designed the set - a magnificent and very professional-looking set - for the 1957 King's Week Festival production of *Twelfth Night* in which I had played my lacklustre Olivia.

Malcolm was - as I later came to recognise - a courageously flamboyant homosexual (he died, sadly, in middle age in 1978, shortly after being elected a full Fellow of Corpus Christi, Cambridge). He would never have tampered with a schoolboy, but at the same time he liked to entertain small groups of senior boys (especially if they were actors), and he took the view that school rules existed to be broken. (He knew, of course, that he had Fred's tacit support over this.) He would secure an innocuous *exeat* for a group of us to have 'tea' with him; tea became drinks, drinks became dinner at The Falstaff, and the guests would roll back to their houses hours after the permitted time, slightly tipsy and surprisingly well-informed on a range of topics which were clearly not on the school curriculum. Even in free-thinking Cambridge Malcolm's style could raise a few eyebrows, and among the more conservative housemasters at King's it provoked apoplexy.

By my time at King's in the latter part of the '50s the school's rough period was over, and Fred was credited - with considerable justice - with making it one of the best schools in the country. There is no doubt that he worked very hard for the institution and that its reputation was buoyant, but Fred's personal vanity was never far from what he was planning or achieving. He saw himself as some sort of academic Oxford grandee *manqué*. Take for example the Shirley Hall: a really preposterously pretentious and lamentably inefficient building. One can see that it was supposed to look like the hall of an Oxford college and that it was also supposed to have been designed so that school stage productions and orchestral concerts could take place in it, but from the day it was opened it was clearly hopelessly ill-suited to both of these latter functions. What it did do well was to provide a show-case for Fred: a grand space in which he could waft up the aisle, ascend the stage and then turn and dominate the assembled pupils from his central dais. Fred wanted Grandeur; flexibility, good acoustics, scenery flies and so forth had all been scrapped in the planning in the cause of Grandeur. And Fred passionately wanted Grandeur in the form of Royalty to come for the Shirley Hall's ceremonial opening. An absurd row - which got a good deal of publicity in the national press - between Fred and the Red Dean, communist Hewlett Johnson (who was then well over 80), over whether King's boys were to be allowed to visit the Dean for tea or not, blew up shortly before the opening of the hall. Fred convinced himself, and often said, that but for that adverse publicity he would have succeeded in obtaining the Queen rather than the Queen Mother for the opening ceremony. Somehow he managed to present it as having been all Hewlett Johnson's fault; he seemed oblivious of the fact that the row, the adverse publicity and the absence of the Queen were direct consequences of his own desire to bully the old man in the Deanery.

The truth is that Worksop, of which he had been headmaster before he came to Canterbury, had not been grand enough, and he managed to make King's into something *fairly* grand but still not quite grand enough. He had a Trollopean (Anthony, not Joanna) desire for status conferred by a particular kind of 'establishment' ivy-clad splendour. He permitted several somewhat unscrupulous stratagems to enhance the school's ratings. Take my own case. My entrance scholarship to the school was in arts subjects, and the regimen to which I and other arts King's Scholars were subjected was exclusively designed to get us scholarships into Oxford or Cambridge colleges. All this was at considerable educational cost: I and my contemporaries in the arts fifth form studied no science at all, ever. At the end of my first year in the school I took O levels (at the age of fourteen) and was then, in effect, doing A level work for *four years* as part of the grooming of a runner in the Oxbridge scholarship race.

Fred seldom relaxed his taste for theatrical effect. He once subjected the whole school, all 600 of us, to a violent harangue - a storm-force jeremiad, which gave full vent to the old ham actor in him - on the subject of 'wenching'. (To be seen talking to, or to have been said to have been seen talking to, a girl from the town came under the heading of 'wenching', and was therefore punishable by beating in Fred's view.) In his brand-new vulgar Shirley Hall he declaimed: "There is one part of the human body which none of you is able to control."

There was a long pause and we waited - of course - to see what word Fred would choose for 'penis'. But he came out with: "The *tongue. Gossip* does more potential damage to this school than anything else." It was beatifully timed, pure Joe Orton farce, and Fred was clearly revelling in the effect he had created.

After I left school I often used to go down to Canterbury in the Cambridge vacations to visit Fred. Retirement didn't suit him. He had shrunk. The towering monster had been replaced by a coughing, chain-smoking, hunched and grumpy toad-shaped figure who knew - I think - that the years left to him were all too few. He was, of course, still in his house in the Precincts and not at ease with his lot. Of his successor he would say, "It's intolerable, impossible. Every morning I look out of my window and I see *that man* going off to *my job*." I once went to see him and had to tell him that I could only stay for 20 minutes before lunching with S S Sopwith, my former housemaster, who had by then retired. The old Fred came back. The eyes bulged with indignation behind the pebble lenses, the rather full, female lips pursed themselves up into a purplish bud of disparagement: "*Sopwith!* Sopwith has *far* more time than I do. I'm a very busy man [with the implication that he had engineered a window in his crowded schedule for that week in honour of my visit!]. You don't need to go and see *Sopwith*." And then he said (with a wholly uncharacteristic vulnerability, like the sudden disappointment of a small child when the party has stopped too abruptly): "Why can't you stay and talk to me?"

127

Charles Powell

Sir Charles Powell was a Canterbury Cathedral chorister and in 1955 moved from its Choir School to the King's School. He went on from there to New College, Oxford, where he achieved a First in history, and in 1963 entered the Diplomatic Service. From 1983 to 1991 he was Private Secretary to the Prime Minister (Margaret Thatcher and subsequently John Major). He is currently a director of Jardine Matheson Holdings and associated companies and of National Westminster Bank, chairing its International Advisory Board.

As a Canterbury Cathedral chorister I saw a bit of John Shirley before I went to King's. We choirboys saw him as an imposing, remote and rather sinister residentiary Canon, the most redoubtable member of a somewhat eccentric Chapter, headed by Dean Hewlett Johnson (whose violent sermons against the Americans over alleged use of poisonous gas in Korea I vividly remember). The Choir School lay on the route through the Precincts between Shirley's house and his headmaster's study. With that curious sphinx-like smile of his, he became a familiar figure to us as he went back and forth. Most of us went on from the Choir School to King's and heard the stories that filtered down about its powerful headmaster. We knew that he had taken over King's 20 years before under somewhat unusual circumstances, which led to his being expelled from the Headmasters' Conference, and that he had a fearsome reputation for demanding the best - be it of the 1st XV or in the academic sphere - and for not tolerating failure. We were equally aware that the school was forging ahead under his strong and single-minded leadership.

When I joined King's, having been Head Boy of the Choir School, I was recognisable to Shirley. My dominant first memories are of his ability to strike fear into the hearts of 650 boys attending Assembly in the Chapter House (the Shirley Hall was still a few years off), as he forced miscreants for smoking, unauthorised absence or other offences to identify themselves in front of the whole school. Occasionally too there would be a 'pep talk'. It was an early lesson for me in the importance of personality in leadership. I have seen it time and time again in life, particularly during my years working for Margaret Thatcher: a really strong personality able to inspire action and success in others whether by affection, fear or example. In truth Shirley had an extraordinarily positive, galvanising effect on the school and on a lot of its boys.

Shirley set out to make King's the 'number one' music school in Britain with its first-class orchestra and the King's Week festival. He determined that we should be pre-eminent in sport (and was not above, as I recollect, keeping boys back beyond the normal leaving age in order to have a good second row forward or a reliable full-back). By the end of the 1950s we were regularly coming in the top three or four of the Oxford and Cambridge scholarship tables, vying with Eton, Manchester Grammar School, Winchester and St Paul's. Even in those days I sensed that all this achievement was being won by a man who was willing to stretch the rules to breaking point and beyond to accommodate his ambitions for the school and to secure the best. And, given that King's was not a school usually spoken of in the same breath as Eton, Winchester, Harrow or Westminster, he did a huge amount to raise its status and allow it to qualify for consideration in the same league.

My choir school background - knowledge of the Cathedral services and the ritual - may have given me some edge with Shirley over my contemporaries. For instance, he was rather keen on the use of incense and he would get me to perform this function in the crypt. The practice was not one approved by the rest of the Chapter; it was as though I was engaged in a subversive activity on his behalf, as I collected the censer from him of an evening and went on my mission to swing it around.

During my middle and later years at King's I went to see him quite frequently, summoned by his notes. One was always rather fearful in anticipation: was it the prelude to being dressed down for some offence? Usually it turned out to be an opportunity for him to talk about the awfulness of the other canons or to relay something indiscreet about another boy or a member of staff. On these occasions he was very free in what he said, talking to you as though you were a fellow adult. This helped build my self-confidence and ambition. Those of us who came from the Choir School, with so much time spent on music, were academically well behind others in our year and had much catching up to do. These chats were a means by which I was inspired to set my sights high. There is little doubt that he had his favourites and some of us were closer to him than others, but I do not recall that this affected our relationships with our contemporaries; perhaps the occasional scornful remark came our way, but no more.

Shirley was one of those flinty headmasters who believed in the utility of a good thrashing. He did not have the repute of Chenevix-Trench in this area but, if not in the beaters' first division, he was fairly high up in the second. The legends were perhaps more alarming than the actuality: we used to hear stories from before my time of the 1st XV being caned for losing a match and that sort of thing. He clearly relished the terror which he could strike in pupils. There would be a written summons to his study in the school and a morning spent sweating and wondering what offence had been committed, and then on your going in he would look up from his desk with a strange grin, difficult to divine, and you would then be sent away. I am not suggesting he was a sadist, but he toyed with people and relished the power which he could exercise over impressionable young boys.

After I left King's, I did not go back until invited to give a talk in 1991 (though I was back in the Precincts for the Channel Tunnel treaty ratification by Mrs Thatcher and President Mitterrand in the Chapter House and, on a separate occasion, the *Herald of Free Enterprise* memorial service in the Cathedral). I left with no overwhelming affection for the school, but it had done a great deal for me and got me to Oxford. Looking back now, it is clear that it was presided over by a great headmaster. Among public school headmasters from Arnold onwards, Shirley should surely rank in the top category as one with the capacity to transform. He picked up King's from almost nothing and developed it into a great school with a distinguished academic and musical record. He understood the psychology of boys and could frighten and inspire them, using the one technique to effect the other - not necessarily the nicest way to proceed but one which brought him tremendous success. It is hard to imagine Shirley in any other role than headmaster and Canon: indeed if one had to go to the drawing-board and design a prototype headmaster for those days, then Shirley would surely be the result. But he was definitely of another generation and no headmaster would succeed today in running a school in such a tyrannical manner. Yet what he achieved at King's has remained.

And his influence on me? He inspired a not particularly bright and not particularly personable boy into achieving a state scholarship to Oxford and getting me to strive for what I had previously deemed unattainable. He had a unique personality skilled in bringing out the very best from those in whom he believed. I was fortunate to have been one of them.

Retirement in 1962: with the Queen Mother and Mrs Shirley.
Photo: Kent Messenger Group.

Michael Morpurgo

Michael Morpurgo became a pupil at the King's School, Canterbury, in 1957 and left in 1962. He was Captain of School in his (and John Shirley's) final year there. Subsequently he went to Sandhurst and King's College, London, and taught English for ten years, two of them at Milner Court (the Junior King's School). He is the author of over 50 children's books, four of which have been filmed and for which he wrote the screenplays. His writing has won him the Whitbread Prize in 1995 and the Writers' Guild Award, the Smarties Award and the Children's Book Award in 1996.

When I am made to think about it, and writing this piece makes me think about it, I am forced to come to the conclusion that I was not at all well educated in the narrowest sense of that word. I went into King's in 1957, academically ordinary and intellectually dull; and in 1962 I came out much the same. I had grown older but I hadn't done much growing up. I had proved myself competent, just about, on the rugby field, and a songster of only modest tunefulness in Edred Wright's choir. An all-round good egg, I shuffled off somewhat unthinkingly to Sandhurst, a place where good eggs of very little brain often go, when they can't think of anything better to do. Why then should I look back on my years at King's as amongst the most intense, the most enriching of my life?

In part it was certainly the place. To live for five years under the shadow of that glorious Cathedral, to walk up the Dark Entry on a summer's evening and out onto the Green Court, to take communion in the Norman Crypt early on Sunday mornings, to hear the night watchman sing out outside your dormitory window, to tread the lush turf of Birley's, and loll along the banks at Plucks Gutter: certainly it was the place.

But it was more the people than the place, I think. I was nurtured throughout by some of the most remarkable people I've known. I had Richard Roberts as my housemaster - always fair, never strident. I had S S Sopwith for my tutor - sherry and pipesmoke in Lardergate once a fortnight. A kind man, wise and honest in all he said. I had Colin Fairservice to coach me on the cricket field and the rugby field. No histrionics, but endless patient encouragement. And then there was Edred Wright whose greatest gift was not just to cultivate the talented but to inspire the rest of us as well. If these men were the cloisters, the quire, the nave of the cathedral of my youth, then Bell Harry Tower was Fred.

The man was a legend long before I went to King's. As new boys we all knew the stories. It was comic-strip stuff. Old worn-out town with a bad name, a no-hope place that badly needed a new sheriff. They found one. He rode into town in his black wide-brimmed hat, packing a Bible, a gun and a cheque-book, and he sorted the place out. Twenty-five years later he'd turned it into the finest town in the territory, a place where every citizen could fulfil his potential. Fred was our very own Wild Bill Hickock, and you didn't mix with him, not if you'd got any sense.

I met this legend for the first time in my first week at the school. He was coming across the Green Court with his gown flying, saw me, pointed at me and called me over. "Mmm," he said, "Morpurgo. Know your father." He prodded me in the stomach. "White belly. Do your jacket up. White belly. Do it up." It wasn't an auspicious start.

It was probably because he was a legend that he was so awesome to a small boy. His appearance was legendary too - always immaculate, shoes shining, suit meticulously worn, bands crisply white, and that hat! His face, very often smiling, was essentially kind. Nothing there to fear. But he was mercurial. Sweetness and light in assembly one day, thunderous and judgmental the next. You never knew.

Then there was the tea party at Number 15, half a dozen of us, and Mrs Shirley and Fred. Here we could talk to the great man for the first time - well, he could talk to us. There was much shifting in seats, and clearing of throats. We offered scones to each other, rather ostentatiously I suspect, and tried not to drop crumbs on the carpet. He beamed a lot, like the sun shining down on young strawberry plants - pleased with the way they were coming on.

As the years passed and our meetings became more frequent, the early awe gave way to admiration, and then affection. I was there when he stormed out of rehearsals for *Othello* - I can't remember why. I was there when he gave us all a half-day because the 1st XV had beaten Dulwich College. I was there when he talked of dying and made me think of it for the first time - a boy called Russell had just died, of cancer I believe. He had the gentle touch, he had the sound and fury. He was a complete communicator.

For some reason best known to himself, he rang me up at home and asked me to be Captain of School. It was to be his last year and my last year. It was to be a roller-coaster of a year, a year during which I would come to know and understand the man, not well, but better. We met almost daily in his office overlooking the Green Court, and when we couldn't meet he'd leave me cards in my pigeon-hole. I had to see to it that support for the 1st XV was more vocal. That everyone dismounted going through the Lattergate arches. That more should turn up for communion. That boaters had to be *worn* in town, not carried. These suggestions I passed on to the assembled school with as much force as I could muster. But his favourite method of keeping me on my toes was to send me cards with nothing on them but biblical references. 'S.Matthew 5 v 5.' He would simply sign them 'F.J.S.' and leave me to puzzle out their implications. I'm still trying to puzzle them out, but I think that was the idea.

We parted on Speech Day, me in court dress and purple gown, Fred in his suit and his bands, and his hat. His handshake was close, as close to a hug as could be allowed. It was a long and silent handshake, and I shan't forget it.

I stumbled after I left King's and almost fell. I was not the person I thought I was, or anyone thought I was. I had a lot more growing up to do. Fred was there during the darkest times, and by that time he had become more than any old headmaster, he had become a friend. He christened my first son, Sebastian, sparkled briefly in retirement, and then died too soon, too young.

He did an extraordinary thing. He made a school where people believed in you - that was his genius. From him came the conviction that built self-belief, self-worth. I left King's with those things in abundance, believing I could make a difference, make a contribution - that was my real education - and so did thousands of us. We have much to thank him for.

"The world needs men like Fred Shirley. We are the poorer today for being so afraid to let exceptional men have their rein - and reign".